MW00964624

The PRAYING Parent

The PRAYING Parent

Making a Lasting Difference in Your Kids' Lives

Debbie Salter Goodwin

Beacon Hill Press of Kansas City
Kansas City, Missouri

Copyright 2005
by Debbie Salter Goodwin and Beacon Hill Press of Kansas City

ISBN 083-412-176X

Printed in the
United States of America

Cover Design: Paul Franitza

All Scripture quotations not otherwise designated are from the *Holy Bible,
New International Version*® (NIV®). Copyright © 1973, 1978, 1984 by International Bible Society. Used by permission of Zondervan Publishing House.
All rights reserved.

Permission to quote from the following additional copyrighted versions of
the Bible is acknowledged with appreciation:

The *New Revised Standard Version* (NRSV) of the Bible, copyright 1989 by
the Division of Christian Education of the National Council of the Churches of Christ in the USA. All rights reserved.

The Message (TM). Copyright © 1993, 1994, 1995, 1996, 2000, 2001, 2002.
Used by permission of NavPress Publishing Group.

Scripture quotations marked KJV are from the King James Version.

Library of Congress Cataloging-in-Publication Data

Goodwin, Debbie Salter.
    The praying parent : making a lasting difference in your kids' lives / Debbie Salter
Goodwin.
        p. cm.
    ISBN 0-8341-2176-X (pbk.)
    1. Parents—Prayer-books and devotions—English. I. Title.

    BV4529.G66 2005
    248.3'2'085—dc22

                                                              2005002556

10 9 8 7 6 5 4 3 2 1

Dedicated to
Lisa Kay Goodwin,
the only one who makes me a mother.
You are all gift to me, a surprise package full of joys and challenges. Both have sent me to my knees in gratitude and for help. It is from those places of surrender and celebration that I have learned these lessons.
It is because of you that I don't forget them.

Contents

How to Use This Book

This book will be as helpful as the prayers it leads you to pray. To push you in the right direction, there are several ways to use it as a tool both to learn how to pray as well as to do the work of praying.

1. Purchase a blank book and make it a prayer journal. Write down the prayers you pray based on principles in this book. Date them. Leave room to note specific answers. Use it to chronicle the changes in you and in your child.

2. Purchase a small notebook and divide it into sections, one for each child. Write sentence prayers based on the principles and scriptures of this book. Date them. Leave room for recording answers.

3. Use the book with a parents' prayer group. Go through the book slowly enough to make yourselves accountable for each lesson. Leave time to pray. Share answers with each other. Don't be surprised if the first answers occur as changes in yourselves before there are changes in your children.

4. Plan to read or review the principles and prayers of this book at least once a year. Use it to evaluate your personal journey with prayer. How have your responses changed because of the prayers you have prayed? What have you learned about God? How is prayer an integral part of your spiritual growth?

5. Write out your scriptural prayers for your children. Enter them into a bound journal and present them to your child on an important occasion: graduation, leaving for college, getting married, and so on.

Acknowledgments

This has been a book on a journey. Many have influenced that journey. My first editor, Jeanette Gardner, shared a bigger vision for my original ideas. Bonnie Perry, director of Beacon Hill Press of Kansas City, has been my patient publisher. When Lisa's heart surgery put all writing projects on hold, Bonnie waited. When an unexpected move to Portland ate big chunks of my writing time, she waited. When Lisa faced another five-month health crisis, she waited. Bonnie, you are every writer's dream publisher. Current editor Judi Perry took my words from manuscript to printed page. Thank you for addressing each detail while keeping the big picture in your head better than I could.

There is another person whose profound influence on my personal journey weaves its way through this book. As a young woman in her first career position, I served on staff with Glaphré Gilliland and sat under her rich teaching on prayer. They were anchor lessons for me. She helped me understand that prayer is more about who God is than what I want.

Family is always an integral part of every writing project. My husband, Mark, pushed, encouraged, counseled, read, listened, and celebrated at each step toward the finished product. Thank you. You are the love of my life, and I will always write better with you beside me.

To extended family, friends, writing colleagues, accountability sisters, thank you for your constant prayers and generous encouragement. I offer these pages as the only way I say thank you.

Dear God,

How do I give my children what they need the most? I watch birthday and Christmas presents lose favored status, wear out, and end up in the trash or a garage sale. I don't want to spend time and money on gifts that don't last. Even good parenting skills aren't enough. Is there anything that will make a lasting difference?

Waiting to Hear

Dear Waiting,
Will you pray?

The God Who Hears

1

Prayer: The Gift That Lasts

Prayer seeks the presence of God
and releases the power of God.
—Stormie Omartian, *The Power of a Praying Parent*

"Inoperable cancer," the doctor said. The words hung like flies permanently caught in a spider web. Kay, 30-year-old wife and mother, could not disengage herself from the death grip of the diagnosis. What about Lisa, her 18-month-old daughter? As a mother, she had applauded Lisa's first words, cheered her first steps, laughed at her first expressions, and enjoyed the emergence of her unique and delightful personality. There was so much of this little girl's life ahead and so little of her own left.

In what would become the last three months of Kay's life, she prayed often for Lisa. She prayed that she would come to know God in a special way. She especially prayed that Lisa would lose her traumatic insecurities demonstrated by an unrelenting fear of the church nursery.

When Kay died, she took her dreams for future motherhood with her—but she left her prayers with God. Prayer is the gift that does not die. I know, because I stepped into the circle of love from which Lisa came when I married Lisa's father. I became Lisa's "new" mother. I have been first-person witness to the answers of Kay's prayers for Lisa. For example, Lisa developed a spiritual sensitivity early in direct contrast to increasing learning problems. In addition, God gave Lisa an abundant sense of security, which she has needed in her life that has been limited by a tangled set of disabilities. I thank God for Kay's prayers, because I have had the opportunity to build upon them. I have never been more convinced that prayer is the most important gift we can give our kids. The prayers we pray stay in God's heart forever. They never die.

Too many of us are novices when it comes to prayer. We're kindergarten students dealing with high school trigonometry problems when we barely know basic arithmetic. At least that's what it feels like. When the stakes are high and we know we must depend on prayer to make a difference, do we know how to make that difference through prayer?

From the beginning, Old Testament and New Testament writers attributed many things to prayer:

- Isaac prayed about his wife's barrenness, and she became pregnant (Gen. 25:21).
- David prayed about the plague devastating Israel, and the plagues stopped (2 Sam. 24:25).
- Hezekiah prayed about the illness that threatened his life, and God healed him (2 Kings 20:5).
- Isaiah prayed for protection from Israel's enemy, and God took care of the enemy (2 Chron. 32:20-21).

These prayers resulted in changed circumstances, restored health, and gave protection from enemies. They came from people who believed that God had right answers to the cries of their hearts. That certainly covers the ground we cross in parenting.

However, nowhere does Scripture tell us that we control the answers to our prayers for our children or ourselves. Nowhere does the Bible promise that we can obtain a detailed printout to tell us how circumstances will change if we pray. Instead, the Bible encourages us to pray often, always, and without ceasing (1 Thess. 5:17).

To be honest, crisis sends me to prayer more quickly than anything else. It's when nothing is working that I think about praying. Unfortunately, when I can think of something to try to solve a problem or relieve a situation, I usually try it before prayer. I look back over my years of parenting, and I cringe to remember when I spoke or acted before I prayed. I worried before I prayed. I looked in a book or called a friend before I prayed.

If I really believe that prayer makes the biggest difference, shouldn't I pray first?

What do you do first?

When your child has a problem, what is your first response? Prioritize the following list based on what you actually do most of the time, not on what you wish you did.

___ Talk about the problem.

___ Talk about your child with a friend.

___ Worry about what will happen.

___ Blame someone for the problem.

___ Pray about what your first response should be.

___ Take a guilt trip over your shortcomings as a parent.

___ Seek advice from a friend.

___ Read or reread a book on parenting.

___ Lecture your child about what he or she should do.

___ Look for wisdom from God's Word.

Another Question

When your child is in some difficulty and you come to the place of praying, what is the focus of your prayer? Do any of your prayers start like this?

Lord, don't let . . .

Why did this have to happen?

What are we going to do if . . . ?

Do you know what the problem with those prayers is? They all focus on circumstances. Nothing breeds more fear than focusing on circumstances. That's because we have no control over circumstances. The choices our children make often create circumstances outside of our control. Or someone else's choice creates a circumstance we can't change. Accidents and health changes are other forms of circumstances that we can't manipulate. What do we do then? How do we pray in the face of circumstances we can't control?

Instead of focusing on the destructive details from circumstances, we need to focus on God. We need to pray the questions that will bring us transformational answers. We need to pray transformational questions. We need to ask God, *What do you need from me? How can I pray for this? How can I change my attitude about this? How do you want me to help?* God will always answer those questions, because the answers will transform us. Besides, the answers to those questions will make more difference than anything a mere circumstance can bring about.

Praying Transformational Questions

Transformational prayers ask questions that obedience answers. They don't accuse anyone. They don't focus on circumstances. They can't be answered with new information about circumstantial changes. When you're ready to obey, you will pray questions that God will answer with instructions that only you can follow.

Examples

What do you need me to do now?
What is the next step?
What will make a difference?
How can I do what you want?
How can I help the most?
How can I stay calm or endure or be quiet or speak the truth in love?
How do you want me to pray for this?
How can I pray in cooperation with your will?

What transformational question do you need to be praying right now?_____

_____

_____

Contrary to what some think, we don't pray to change our children. We pray to change ourselves. Our changed attitudes and actions can influence changes in our children's responses and decisions. However, it isn't always immediate, nor does it always happen the way we want.

Why Pray?

We know that the Bible tells us to pray. We know that prayer is the right thing to do. But do we know why? I've talked to parents who innocently ask, "If God knows everything that will happen, how can my prayer make a difference?" That's a circumstance-based question. The answer to why we pray isn't about circumstances. It's about transformation—our transformation first. That's why we need to review the following key principles.

1. Prayer connects me to the one who knows everything.

As parents, we don't like to admit that we don't know everything. Some days it feels as if we know nothing. Since God knows everything, we need Him to tell us what we need to know or do. No one else sees the whole picture. No one else understands how our part fits into a bigger scheme. No one else sees the end from the beginning. It's an exercise in futility to pretend that our partial and completely limited information is enough to make a difference in our children's lives. We need God's all-knowing direction.

It's easier to depend on our human knowledge: what we think or feel or have experienced. However, when we do, we risk allowing something other than trust in God to control our actions and reactions. It could be fear, a desire to control, a need to be accepted, or a host of other insecurities that can influence our perceptions and our actions. That's why we need the connection to the only one who knows everything. That's why we pray.

God knows everything. He doesn't get any of His information from us or any other counselor. While we can't know everything God knows, He'll share wisdom with us. However, there's a stipulation. We must be obedient and discerning if we're to receive His wisdom. Remember James 1:6? We can't come to God ex-

---

What do the following scriptures say that God knows?

Isa. 40:14 *God didn't have to consult anyone because he knows everything.*

Rom. 11:33-36 *For from him and through him & to him are all things*

Dan. 2:21-22 *He controlls everything He gives wisdom & knowledge*

---

pecting to pick and choose what we like from what He tells us. We must always operate on a prior commitment to obey whatever He says.

It's not that we forget that God knows everything. We just don't act on that knowledge. We parent our children through school problems, dating problems, marriage problems, and job problems. Again and again, we realize that we don't know everything. That's what scares us. Out of fear we struggle to know just a little more than we do. Actually, the only information we need is a correct understanding of what's *really* happening. While we can collect facts about a situation or a person, we can't always verify motives. We continue to bump into what we don't know.

Praying for our boys has taught me
a lot about trust and surrender.

—Gary Sivewright

Of course, we pray about it. We want God to add some specific knowledge to our information. We want to know if Susie is going to get Mrs. Dunn as her second-grade teacher. We want to know if John will get the promotion he needs. However, prayer is not simply a way to get new information. In fact, one of the first things we need to do when we pray is surrender our need to know the future. That very act of submission connects us to everything God knows. Of course, that doesn't mean that God will tell us what we think we want to know. He promises to tell us what we can obey. That's all He has ever asked of us: to obey what we know. It should comfort us to realize that we don't have to know something more. We just have to obey. We rest in the knowledge that God knows, and because He knows, we don't have to. What He understands about your child is always correct. His perceptions are never off base.

Applying this understanding to prayer means that I ask myself, *Does God have enough knowledge to deal with this crisis or difficulty?* When I remind myself that He does, then I don't have to know any more than He reveals. When I pray to the one who knows everything, He provides me with discerning wisdom that helps me pray for the true need of my child. He protects me from praying just to remove the symptoms of a problem. He guides me to pray based on the realities that He sees even when they're different from the ones I see.

> Lord,
>   We're glad you're our Father. When we come to you with things we don't understand about our children, you understand. We thank you for your Word and the way it guides us in dealing with our children. You give us the wisdom we need just when we need it, and we rejoice. We're privileged to call you Father and to know that we can bring our concerns to you.
>
> > Grateful for your wisdom,
> > A mother leaning on you,
> > Ina Strait

For Example

What if I'm concerned that my son or daughter is getting involved in a relationship with the wrong person? First of all, as I remember that God knows everything, I must also acknowledge that He knows what made my child desperate for this companionship. Recognizing that He knows what I don't know motivates me to ask Him for the wisdom to discern my child's true need. The true need may be insecurity, poor self-esteem, desire for acceptance. While I may not be able to meet that need, I can cooperate with God's ways for meeting that need. Furthermore, when I focus on a true need, I'll be less likely to respond in ways that push my child to embrace the wrong relationship more deeply.

The First Critical Prayer

Protect my mouth from speaking anything but your wisdom.
May my attitudes reflect that you know what I do not.
Protect me from responding out of fear about the situation.
Help me demonstrate my confidence in your all-knowledge.
Give me insight into the true needs of my child as you see them.
Help me develop the relationship that encourages my child to talk about needs.

2. Prayer connects me to the only one who loves my child more than I do.

Parental love is strong. It makes a grown man make crazy faces and play with bunny rabbits just to get a smile from his new baby. It makes mothers stay up all night and not complain about it. It produces superhuman strength when a child's life depends on it.

And where did parental love come from? Who was the first parent? God, of course. We can love our children only as deeply as we have learned that God loves us.

God's love is an everlasting love that draws us to Him. It's a lavish, undeserved love that makes us His children. It's not an assumed love—it's a demonstrated love. God gave us the best evidence of His love when He gave His Son to be a complete model and message of His deep love.

Describe God's love with the following verses:

Jer. 31:3 _____

_____

1 John 3:1 _____

_____

1 John 4:9 _____

_____

Rom. 8:35-39 _____

_____

We Can Trust His Love

I'll never forget the look of absolute horror on a mother's face when I talked about trusting my daughter completely to God. "I could never do that," she said as if I had just suggested abusive treatment. She really believed that no one else, including God, could defend, protect, explain, instruct, or nurture her child the way she could. After all, she was the mother. Isn't mother love strong enough to do it all?

I think most of us realize that parental love has its limits. But do we realize that God's love does not? Do we really believe that God's love is kind, lavish, relational, demonstrative, stable, powerful, and never fails? As we take our children to God in prayer, we take them to the one who loves them better and more deeply and more perfectly than we ever could. What a relief! If my child's spiritual growth and maturity depends on my love expressing itself perfectly all the time, we're in big trouble. And so are you.

The good news is that it doesn't. The one who demonstrates the nature, meaning, and ways of love, loves our children *with* us, *through* us, and sometimes *for* us. The question is *Can you trust that God's love is enough to make a difference in whatever your child faces?* We take our children to God through prayer to remind ourselves that we're not our children's last hope. God loves them so much more than we do. Prayer helps us find the way to cooperate with a love bigger than our own.

3. Prayer connects me to the one who has all resources to help.

I'm always brainstorming. I feel that I need options when I face a difficult situation. That's a strength *and* a weakness. As a strength, it protects me from tunnel vision. But as a weakness, it tempts me to solve problems on my own, asking for God's blessing after I have decided what to do. Instead, I need to pray as a way of reviewing the resources God has at His disposal. I need to be conscious of those unlimited resources as I bring my child to God.

Describe God's problem-solving abilities from the following verses:

Jer. 32:27 _____

_____

Ps. 33:6, 9 _____

_____

Mark 10:27 _____

_____

Eph. 1:19-20 _____

_____

God is a problem-solving God. No problem is too hard for Him. His words were powerful enough to create a whole world. Whatever He does lasts. Impossibilities don't daunt Him. No help we get from anyone else can compare to the problem-solving power God has to share with us. It's the same power that raised Jesus to life. It's always life-giving power.

However, there's a catch. God can trust us with His power and resources only as long as we surrender *all* control. He can't give His answers or power to someone who would misuse them. That means we have to give up our expectations about details, changed circumstances, and timing. It means we can't yield to any part of manipulation.

The question is not *Can God's resources make a difference?* The question is *How does God want to use His resources through me to make a difference?* How does God want to use creation power, resurrection power, and all-things-possible power to make a difference?

Before you pray, ask yourself the following questions.

1. Can I apply Jesus' name to what I'm asking? (Matt. 6:9)
2. Does what I ask connect directly to God's will as revealed in Scripture? (1 John 5:14)
3. Have I released all expectations and control so that God can use me as a channel for His power and resources? (Heb. 12:1)
4. Have I surrendered all time factors to God? (Ps. 31:15)
5. Am I demonstrating changes that God makes in my life so that my child will want to know more about God and His ways? (1 Cor. 11:1)
6. Am I harboring any unforgiveness toward my child or another person that can block God's ability to use me? (Mark 11:25)

Waiting Room Praying

In our instant-gratification society, we want quick fixes and immediate results. Since God does not operate by our timing, His answers to our prayers often send us to waiting rooms. What seems like an emergency to us is not to Him.

Have you watched people pass time in hospital waiting rooms? I have. They sleep, read books, thumb through magazines, make conversation, or stare mindlessly into open space.

They act as if all time and responsibilities have stopped even when some emergency and frenzied activity placed them there.

Waiting for answers to our prayers should not be like hospital waiting rooms. While waiting for God's answers, we don't pass the time doing nothing. Sometimes the lessons we learn during a waiting period are the biggest part of God's answer to our prayer. That means our waiting times should be productive and full. Find a new way to express your love to your child. Resist the temptation to do something in order to get a certain response. It could be as simple as a compliment or as tangible as participating in a child's favorite activity.

Look for your steps of obedience during a waiting time. Ask God to keep your mouth from sin (Ps. 39:1). Ask Him for ways to protect you from worrying or demonstrating any other lack of trust (Phil. 4:6-7). You can also seek out a friend with whom you can share your concern. Rather than talking about the problem, ask your friend for guidance about the way you're focusing your prayer. Talk more about God than about the problem.

Another very important part of a waiting period can be the prayers you pray for yourself. Whatever you're asking God to do in the life of your child, ask Him to meet a similar need in your own life. If you're asking God to help your child make right decisions, pray it for yourself as well. If you're asking God to protect your child from temptation, ask it for yourself as well.

What can I do while I wait for an answer to prayer?

1. I can surround my child with love.
2. I can affirm my child's strengths.
3. I can look for my part of obedience.
4. I can seek counsel from another Christian about the focus of my prayer.
5. I can ask God to answer in my life whatever I'm praying for in the life of my child.

---

*The most important lesson I have learned
about praying for my children is God's
sense of timing and learning to wait.*

—Ina Strait

Why pray? We pray to remind ourselves that God knows everything, loves more deeply than we can, and has more resources to make a difference than anything we can do alone. We pray to find what obedience God needs from us that will make the biggest difference in the lives of our children. We pray to make eternal deposits into their lives. We pray because nothing else we will ever do will last longer. We pray to give them a gift that will last.

Your Turn

- Go back to "What do you do first?" What do you want your first response to be? How could you remind yourself to respond differently? (Examples: a note on the bathroom mirror or a symbol conspicuously placed.)
- Write down an example of a transformational prayer question you could be praying right now.
- As you pray for your children this week, pray through these questions first:
  1. Do I believe that God's knowledge is more accurate than mine? Where have I acted as if my knowledge was enough?
  2. Can I trust that God's love can make a difference? How can I cooperate more specifically with the way He loves my child?
  3. Am I giving God a pure heart so that He can release His power and resources through me?
- Write a prayer for yourself based on the three principles about God's all-knowledge, all-love, and all-resources. Pray it every day.

My Prayer

With this in mind, we constantly pray for you . . .
that by his power he may fulfill every good purpose
of yours and every act prompted by your faith.
—2 Thess. 1:11

God,

She took her first steps today. It was all giggle and glee for both of us. She wobbled — but she walked. I think she knew I was still within reach, so she risked this independent act. I was clapping and cheering as if she had won a marathon. Help me never lose the exhilaration of watching my child take other necessary first steps in this journey of growing up. Help me be the cheerleader she needs, even when those steps take her away from my reach.

A novice

Dear Novice,
She'll always be
within my reach.

The God Who Is Near

2

Praying for First Times

The beginning is the half of every action.
—Greek proverb

When a baby takes his or her first steps, he or she toddles into a new world. Before standing, he or she found everything on the floor fascinating. Walking children explore a new world with first steps. They discover that shoes have legs. They find that toilets and television buttons are at just the right height. Their new world both excites them and gets them into trouble. Such is the dilemma of first steps.

A baby's first steps are just the beginning of other first times. There's the first day at school, the first sleepover, the first job, the first date. The list never stops. It must continue if we want our children to grow up emotionally healthy.

Most parents don't think to pray for a toddler's first steps unless something seems wrong. When Kathy's daughter's first steps didn't come as expected, Kathy prayed intensely for a first step. The doctor suggested tests to make sure nothing was wrong. Thankfully, the tests showed she was normal. Her daughter just wasn't ready to walk. Today she walks almost as much as she talks. Sometimes Kathy wishes her prayers hadn't been quite so effective.

Does there have to be something wrong before we think to pray about first times? I've come to believe that praying for the first times in life is just as critical as praying during crises. Why? Because the first of something sets a pattern that influences everything that comes after.

Sometimes we move tentatively into first times with our children because we fear what will happen. However, true prayer, the prayer that connects us with the God who knows everything, calms that fear. James reminds us that God will give wisdom generously to anyone who believes that God's wisdom *is* an answer to prayer (James 1:5-6). As parents, we need to believe that God is willing to tell us what we need to know as we shadow our children during their first times.

Don't forget that many of our children's first times become *our* first times too. Every prayer we pray for them must become a boomerang prayer for ourselves as well.

Why Pray for First Times?

1. We pray for first times because they influence direction.

The second day of a new school semester goes a lot better when the first day goes well. The reverse is also true. When children experience a difficult first day, they fear that a second day won't go much better. Negative first experiences can teach a child to be afraid of the new. Or a first experience may introduce children to choices they may not be prepared to make. Since we want our children to grow up confident and prepared for new experiences, we need to pray specifically for them during first times. We need to build into first-time experiences the characteristics that will make them successful in a growth-producing way. Focused prayer during first times helps us accomplish this.

Name a positive first-time experience.	Name a negative first-time experience.
What factors made it positive?	What factors made it negative?

How did this impact a second time?	How did this impact a second time?
Ask God to help you add positive factors to your child's first-time experience.	

First steps should be an exciting adventure of growth and discovery. We pray about them because we want God to direct our children's first steps. We want them to learn the right things from first experiences. We want our participation in their first times to be everything that helps them grow physically, spiritually, and emotionally. The only way we can do that is by learning to pray in a way that helps us listen to God's instructions for *us*.

> *Dear God,*
>   *Today she started kindergarten. I know I should be praying for her, but I find myself coming to you with my needs. I want to learn how to affirm her small beginnings instead of pushing her to the next level. I want to reject every response that ties performance or behavior to my identity. I don't want to prick her helium balloon spirit with any overbearing comment about what she should have done. If she can learn to count and cut, I should be able to learn a few basics too. Since you've been through many beginnings, will you help me through this one so that we can all look back and call it good?*
>   *Relying on your first-time experience,*
>   *A mother in kindergarten too.*
>   *Debbie Goodwin*

2. We pray because we often become our children's coaches during their firsts.

First times introduce new experiences. To help our children find success and overcome their fears of something new, we coach them. New experiences profit from effective coaching.

They don't thrive in negative, critical environments. Early failure, embarrassment, insecurity, rejection, or other negative results can affect our children's desire to try again. That's why first-time experiences make a critical difference. This is true for toddlers entering a new world on their feet. It's true of young adults starting college.

The key word is coaching. When a baby demonstrates readiness to leave the crawling world of rug burns and dirty knees, what do parents do? They become coaches and cheerleaders. A parent will encourage any hint of progress even before it's completed. If a child falls while making this courageous try, a parent gives the child every reason to try again. In first-step coaching, success means making a good attempt. It doesn't always mean reaching the goal.

To coach:

To use words, instruction, demonstration, prompting, and practice to encourage the successful mastery of a new experience.

Good coaches understand the importance of easy-to-follow directions, simple demonstrations, timely prompting, and repeated practice. Good coaches know that it does not involve manipulation, control, lecture, debate, or argument. Good coaches understand that successful small steps are more important than moving too fast. They recognize that affirmation goes a lot farther than criticism. They realize that even a parent-coach can be called on a technical foul for speaking the wrong way at the wrong time.

When have I allowed my parent comments to degenerate into something that was *not* effective coaching?

_____

_____

Perhaps the most important reason we pray about our coaching position in our children's first experiences is that the focus of our prayers will influence the nature of our coaching.

The focus of our prayers will influence the nature of our coaching.

A Helpful Prayer Focus

Sharon requested prayer for her son because he was going to have tubes put in his ears, and he was afraid of this surgery. Even though Sharon was a nurse and knew that the surgery was not serious, she was worried because her son was afraid. I suggested that she pray that her son learn to trust God for the times when his mother could not be with him. Immediately, this prayer focus gave her a new perspective. Her focus influenced her coaching. The fear left. Because she was calm and encouraging, her son became more confident. She was able to help him focus on how God would be with him when she could not. Both learned something important in this first step.

It's easy for us to allow our prayers to focus on our fear in a situation. It could be the fear of letting go, the fear of what will happen, or fear of some other unknown or insecurity. If we focus on our fear, our coaching will probably reflect that fear. We'll push instead of instruct. We'll add pressure instead of encouraging a calm spirit. On the other hand, if our prayers focus on God's ability to direct our children's first steps, we coach with a different confidence. We affirm everything that points our children in the right direction. We encourage, cheer, affirm, listen, and pray from a different perspective. We more nearly reflect the parenting style of our Heavenly Father. The results are much more positive—for both of us.

3. We pray because first times prepare our children for continued development.

When our children are young, we watch for early signs of

An effective coach

1. Has mastered the first-time skill.
2. Understands how to sequence instructions.
3. Affirms attitudes and actions that contribute to learning the skill.
4. Models the skill appropriately.
5. Realizes that positive words help more than negative words.
6. Makes learning fun and productive.

Which effective coaching skill do I need to practice more? __

_____

_____

How can I apply it to a situation now? _____

_____

_____

---

motor and perceptual development because it helps us know when they're ready for the next step of physical development. We should do the same for key steps of spiritual development. If our children aren't prepared spiritually for a new stage of growth and independence, anything from catastrophe to loss of confidence could result.

It's very easy to take a negative detour in our prayers. We don't pray to prevent the problems that *might* happen. Prayers that focus on *what-ifs* are not grounded in reality. God is a God of truth. He comes alongside to help us deal with the realities of a present situation. We pray for discernment to identify our children's readiness. We pray to understand how God wants us to help prepare them for a new step. We pray to prepare ourselves for what their new step means in our lives.

Something follows every beginning. The quality and effectiveness of what follows often depends on the nature of the beginning. When we miss important steps, it will affect the result.

Praying that our children learn the right things in their beginnings prepares them for continued development.

We pray to discern our child's readiness.
We pray to understand how God wants us to help.
We pray to prepare ourselves for the next step.

Somehow it seems easy to address preparation steps with sequential skills like learning to walk, talk, or read. But how do we prepare our children for developing an intimate relationship with God? This kind of preparation is about passing on our understanding of who God is. It's about learning to recognize God's instructions on a daily basis. It's frightening to realize that we can do a good job preparing our children to live successfully in our culture while rendering them ill-prepared for life with God. That's the development issue that sends me to my knees regularly.

To climb steep hills requires slow pace at first.
—William Shakespeare

For Example

One day in a Bible study, the leader challenged us to pray that our children would love to read the Bible for themselves. She explained how dedicated we become in helping our children read and asked us to be as purposeful in encouraging our young readers to read the Bible.

I saw the discrepancy in my own life immediately. Lisa's learning disabilities made reading an exceptionally difficult process for her. I took her to the library, read to her every night before bed, and encouraged her first efforts. Still, she always tested significantly below grade level. While I worked with Lisa every night on her reading ability, I only asked her to *carry* a Bible to church. That's when I began to pray that Lisa would develop a love for reading God's Word. With that prayer focus, I looked for resources that would help. One day I found a Bible storybook with a controlled vocabulary for beginning readers. I bought it for Lisa. Soon it became her favorite book to read because she could read it for herself. It took several more years before she was ready to tackle the Bible; but when she did, I recognized how the first steps of reading Bible stories on her own contributed to her reading the Bible. Today, her Bible is marked up more than mine.

Pray About It

How can you pray for the next first in your child's life?

What skill, confidence, or understanding about God will prepare him or her best? _____

_____

_____

_____

How can you prepare yourself to be ready for your child's next first? _____

_____

_____

_____

How does God want you to coach his or her preparation? __

_____

_____

_____

Spend time in prayer asking Him. Record your answers and insights. _____

_____

_____

Getting Rid of Guilt

While it's our parental responsibility to encourage appropriate growth and development, it's impossible to prepare our children for everything. Too many times we play *shoulda-oughta*. We *should have* done better. We *ought to* have known better. We take guilt trips that are unhelpful detours in our parenting processes. Unfortunately, guilt does not help us pray or parent. It pushes us to enable, rationalize, ignore, or fear.

Guilt pushes us to enable, rationalize, ignore, or fear.

Take a reality check. Maybe you should have recognized the danger signs that could have prevented a problem—but you didn't. That's the reality you must confront. Take that reality to God, and ask Him to evaluate your *shoulda-oughta* list. Confess any disobedience or refusal to listen to Him. Learn how you can be more informed, more in touch, more observant, more available, or more obedient. Let God clear your heart of guilt, because guilt focuses on your own need, not your child's. To become an effective intercessor for your child, you must clear your heart of guilt.

Guilt focuses on your own need, not your child's needs.

Clear Your Heart

- Ask God if you failed to obey, listen, or acknowledge a reality in some way.
- Confess your failures, and receive His forgiveness.
- If it would be a relationship-strengthening action, ask your child to forgive you.
- Ask God for the best way to coach, support, and pray for your child.
- Obey what He says, and see how it opens new possibilities.

Praying for First Times

When our daughter started school, she encountered more than her share of difficult first times because of her complicated mix of learning and physical disabilities. Each first introduced a new crisis. At the beginning, I prayed fearfully from my mother's need to protect her. However, I came to learn that fearful prayers do not produce a peaceful heart. That's when I learned the importance of refocusing my prayers away from the circumstances that overwhelmed me and toward God, who saw everything from a completely different perspective. I wish I could say that this has become my natural reflex to first times. Unfortunately, it hasn't. Again and again, it has to be a conscious choice.

Fearful prayers do not produce a peaceful heart.

The following principles influenced my prayers away from fear. They helped me stay focused on the reality that God is in control. They cleared my heart from unnecessary entanglements. They helped me pray God's will in my life as well as in my daughter's. They still guide my prayers for Lisa in the first times of her new independence.

1. No one understands beginnings better than God.

God is the source of all beginnings, the first of all first things. From His experience with all beginnings, He willingly shares His wisdom with anyone taking first steps and experiencing something new. When we pray with that understanding, we take confidence in what God knows instead of borrowing fear about what we don't know.

The first words of the first verse of the Bible remind me of a most important truth: "In the beginning God created" (Gen. 1:1). Too often we rush to God when we see the first signs of trouble, well after the beginning. God takes great joy in creating the details of His plan from the beginning. Our prayers should focus on giving Him total creative control from the very beginning of any new experience.

Do you remember what God said after each creative act in the beginning? He called it good. God always wants to create His good in beginnings. We need to pray for that same creative good to take place in our children's lives at the very beginning. It's a very powerful prayer.

> *Look at him, Father. So proud. So purposeful. Breaking rank. Accepting the credentials of his success. Wasn't it just yesterday that I gripped his squirming hand and gave him that tour of his first schoolroom? Wasn't it just moments ago when he gave me that dreaded good-bye hug and ran to a waiting school bus? We tried to shelter him from the sticks and stones of society, and now he will be a citizen of its system. First, he was ours alone to teach. Now, others will teach him. Once he thought our way was the only way. Now, he will be told of others. Soon it will be his graduation day, and I bring him to you as I brought him on that first day.*
> *Would that I could physically run to him, grab his hand again, and lead him on a tour of this brave new world. I can't, Father. But you can. I trust your wisdom to be his refuge and your grace to be his strength.*
> > *Gratefully,*
> > *His proud father, Stan Toler*

Where have you borrowed fear about what you don't know instead of relying on God's creative work in a beginning? ___

_____

_____

Pray an "in the beginning" prayer, asking God to create something good. Then start looking for it. _____

_____

_____

2. Pray that your child will obey what he or she already knows.

God starts with what we already know to obey. He knows that it's the best place to begin. Perhaps this is where we fail as parents more than we realize. We're afraid that our children don't know enough. That justifies for us any number of lectures and wordy avalanches trying to push more information into our children so they'll behave better, choose better, relate better, and follow God better. However, more information is useless when we aren't obeying what we already know. Besides, knowledge doesn't motivate obedience; a loving relationship with God does.

Encouraging obedience to God begins with a relationship, not a rule. Children reject rules before they turn away from a relationship. We pray that they'll recognize evidences of God's love in their lives. We pray that they'll find joy in obeying what pleases God. We pray that God-pleasing obedience will mark their first steps and influence good directions.

Describe your child's relationship to God. _____

_____

_____

Where does it need to grow deeper? _____

_____

How does God want you to encourage this growth? Write your prayer. _____

_____

_____

---

3. Pray that your child learns to depend on God in first times.

Children need to know that God coaches and encourages first steps. They need to know how to hear God give His encouraging words. When we teach a preschooler how God takes care of fears about sleeping in a new room, it's an important step of trust for a life journey, filled with many new places.

Do you remember learning the geometry principle that says the shortest distance between two points is a straight line? Our goal in parenting is to nurture a straight line between God and our children. While triangles are helpful in teaching and nurturing, they must give way to straight lines to produce spiritual maturity. Whatever pushes us to strengthen *our* straight-line relationships with God also helps us teach our children to develop their own straight-line relationships.

In intercessory prayer one seldom ends where one began.
—Douglas V. Steere, *Prayer and Worship*

---

4. What God knows will carry your child through what *you* don't know.

You are the primary intercessor for your child, and your prayer focus is critical. Focusing your prayers solely on what *you* know is an incomplete way to pray. No matter how much you know, it will never be enough. That's where connecting to God's all-knowledge breeds confidence and brings peace. Since He knows everything, He knows what you need to know to help your child right now. That's all the information He'll give. The best way to access that information is through prayer.

What happens to your child on the other side of a first-time experience doesn't depend only on what you know or don't know. It does depend on what God knows. No matter what the first step is, it can always lead to God's will. Pray in that direction and with that focus. Remember: your focus will affect your coaching.

5. Offer God your fears without passing them on to your child.

It has happened more than I like to admit. My response to a situation sets the bar for my child's response. If I respond with fear, she responds with fear or one of its close relatives, such as anger, rebellion, or denial. I'm still learning how important it is for me to let God deal with my fears, especially when they're irrational or based on unrealities. Even in the face of unavoidable fear, God communicates His control in a way that can defuse the dangerous repercussions of expressing that fear. That's why it's vitally important to acknowledge and confess your parental fears through prayer.

Celebrate First Times

To make the most of lessons from first-time experiences, find ways to celebrate them:

1. Give a baptism/confirmation party. If God and His angels celebrate this decision in the life of your child, why shouldn't everyone else?
2. Send a card when you recognize key spiritual growth events.
3. Celebrate your child's first camp or first mission trip with a symbolic key to suggest the new doors this first experience opens. Make presenting it part of the celebration.
4. Play the game "The first time I _____" to give your child a chance to hear about your first-time experiences. Then ask your child to share a first-time experience. Talk about the ways they're alike.
5. Plan small celebrations after important firsts of a school year: the first test, the first report, the first practice, and so on. Don't tie them to performance; celebrate the lessons learned.
6. Celebrate seasonal firsts: the first snow, the first garden flower, the first rain, the first sunny day.

Father,
   I'll never forget the consuming joy of cradling my son in my arms. Our hearts seemed as one, the same as when I

carried him within my body. Did I remember to thank you for touching me with the quiet confidence that you had sent a company of angels to his little room?

Now, Father, he has his own room in his own home. And someone dear to me as well holds him in her arms, someone chosen before the stars were, to love him as much now as I loved him then. I ask you to sentry those same messengers around his home. And give me a still assurance that they'll form a heavenly wall against the earthly wiles of those who would destroy the home that you have given him—that place where he'll love others as you love him.

Confidently,
His grateful mother
Linda Toler

Remember: first times set direction. That's why prayer should be an important part of every direction-setting first. While there's always room for midcourse corrections, they sometimes add unnecessary frustration or reversals. Instead, take every beginning to the God of beginnings to see what He wants to create. Then you'll know what to pray for.

Praying for First Times

1. Pray with the understanding that no one understands beginnings better than God (Gen. 1:1).
2. Pray that your child will obey what he or she already knows (Phil. 1:6; 2 Tim. 3:14).
3. Pray that your child learns to depend on God in first times (Phil. 1:9; Eph. 1:18).
4. Pray that God will carry your child through what you don't know (Isa. 46:10; Jer. 29:11).
5. Offer God any fear you have about your child's first-time experience so that you won't pass fear on to your child (Gen. 26:24; Exod. 14:13).

Your Turn

- Ask God to teach you how to be the coach and encourager your child needs. Read Exod. 4:12-14: How did Moses "coach" the people he cared about?
- Ask God himself to be your child's coach. What are God's qualifications according to Isa. 43:13?
- Ask God to help you identify your child's key first-time experiences. Then ask Him to order the first steps of those experiences. What do Ps. 5:8 and 37:23 remind us about God's skill in ordering steps?
- Ask God to empower your child to make confident, productive, and God-pleasing first steps. What are some of these results according to Ps. 37:4-5 and Matt. 6:33?

He who began a good work in you
will carry it on to completion.
—Phil. 1:6

Dear God

I can't think of anything I want more for my children than for them to know you, accept you, and live for you. I don't want my children to settle for a good life when they can have eternal life. But there are so many crossroads ahead. What more can I do?

Fearful

Dear Fearful,
Live your salvation, and let me reach your children through you.

The God Who Never Stops Reaching

3
Praying for Salvation

Salvation is the real business of life.
—C. S. Lewis

There is no prayer more important than the prayer for our children's salvation. That prayer, more than any other, connects us with God's heart. We never have to wonder about His will in the matter. Every act of God's heart from the beginning of time has been to bring His children to himself, to establish an intimate relationship, and to provide for their well-being forever. If we're to be the parents God calls us to be, we need to reflect His heart from the very beginning of our parenting. We must make our children's salvation our top prayer priority.

A Critical Prayer Priority

This truth impacted my husband and me just in time. Lisa's first four years were difficult. There were seizures at one and a half. She lost her mother to cancer before she turned three. She was diagnosed with juvenile rheumatoid arthritis at five. I became her mother when I married her father three months before the diagnosis. It will come as no surprise that Lisa's physical and emotional struggles became our intense prayer targets.

One night after we had settled her in bed and retreated to the living room for what had become our special time to pray, my husband, Mark, shared something that changed our prayer focus from that day on. He talked about how many prayers we had been praying for Lisa's health in comparison to how few prayers we had prayed for her spiritual well-being. We agreed to pray *first* for Lisa's spiritual health before we prayed about a physical issue.

Here's what I learned. God gave me the sensitivity to see how He was working in Lisa's life in direct proportion to my prayers for her salvation. I remember telling Mark one day that I believed Lisa was nearing a time when she would make her own profession of faith. I started watching for it, expecting it, praying for it. I'll never forget the night Lisa asked Jesus to take away her sin and make her completely His child. Not only did I thank God for her decision—I thanked Him that He had opened the eyes of my heart in a way that I could see it coming.

Bolstered by this wonderful answer to prayer, I wondered what else God would do in Lisa's life if we continued making her spiritual health our priority prayer focus. Perhaps the most obvious answer to our prayer is this: in spite of confusing and paralyzing learning problems, Lisa learned to read and comprehend God's Word better than anything else she read. She always falls way below grade average on a comprehension test, but she astounds people with her insight and understanding of God's Word.

Of course, we continue to pray for Lisa's health issues. However, I've come to understand that the most important place Lisa needs to be healthy and whole is in her relationship to God. It's the only place where health makes an eternal difference.

Why Pray for Salvation?

Too many parents postpone their prayer focus for their child's salvation. We pray for an unborn child's health. We pray for our children's academic development. But we don't always pray specifically for their salvation unless there are signs that a child may be rejecting God and His ways. Perhaps we need to review why praying for salvation is a crucial prayer.

1. Praying for salvation connects us to God's priority for His children.

It should be a relief that we don't have to ask *if* we are to pray for salvation. The Bible clearly answers that issue. The entire story of God is about His plan to bring us to himself. We must be committed to this priority to fulfill our parenting responsibilities by God's standards. Our prayers will show how seriously we give ourselves to that priority.

Although nothing we do will guarantee that our children will accept God's gift of salvation, we can become more sensitive to issues that make a difference. Praying for salvation orders our parenting priorities and protects us from making side issues more important than salvation.

How could you use the following scriptures to shape your salvation prayers for your children?

1 Pet. 1:18-19: _____

_____

_____

Gal. 1:3-5: _____

_____

_____

Acts 4:12: _____

_____

_____

2 Cor. 7:10: _____

_____

_____

God wants to rescue our children from living empty lives. He wants to protect them from experiencing the inevitable consequences of sin. Since there's no other person, activity, or life priority that can offer our children these benefits, their salvation must be a specific focus through prayer.

2. Praying for salvation makes an eternal difference.

Every parent wants to make a difference. However, it's the *eternal* difference that matters. Getting a good teacher, getting good grades, winning sports games, planning fun birthday parties, and taking memorable family vacations have their places—but nothing makes a more lasting difference than salvation.

Review Paul's parent heart. Again and again he opens his heart through his writing to reveal how passionately he worked for and prayed for the salvation of others. As parents, we must ask the question *How passionate am I about my children's salvation?* Everything else I do for my children will eventually end. Salvation is the never-ending gift. Why wouldn't I give it my priority prayer attention?

Pray Paul's prayer by inserting the name of your child in the blank:

My heart's desire and prayer to God for _____ is that he [she] may be saved [Rom. 10:1].

Review Your Salvation Story

As you pray for your children, start by reviewing the meaning of salvation in your own life. Do you understand what you were saved from? While some people have experienced more of sin's consequences and may testify to dramatic contrasts, the key issues of salvation do not depend on how much God has forgiven. They depend on understanding that everyone needs God's salvation. Do you understand what you're saved *for*, and does your life reflect it in growing measures? Think about what would be different if you had not accepted God's gift of salvation. Then, thank God again and again for His indescribable gift. Let your gratitude for God's gift in your life fuel your passion to pass God's plan for salvation on to your children.

*No man ever really finds out what he believes in
until he begins to instruct his children.*

—Anonymous

Write out your salvation story. Use vocabulary that fits your children's ages. Focus on the specific time when you asked Jesus to forgive the ways you turned away from Him. Explain the difference it has made in your life. Review it often. Share it with another Christian parent. Then begin praying for an opportunity to share it with each of your children at the right time.

Writing Your Salvation Story

1. Who influenced your decision to follow Christ?
2. When and how did you recognize your need for salvation?
3. Describe when you asked Jesus to forgive your self-centeredness and decided to follow Him with your attitudes and actions.
4. Explain the difference this decision made in other decisions, relationships, and priorities.
5. What is the biggest benefit you have seen in your life because you followed Jesus?

---

*Always be prepared to give an answer
to everyone who asks you to give the reason
for the hope that you have.*

—1 Pet. 3:15

Just a warning here: children are quick to detect hypocrisy. This is one area in which the actions and attitudes of your daily life must match what you say happened when Jesus took over

My Salvation Story

Before I became a Christian . . .

Then I repented.

Now that I'm a Christian . . .

your life. If you're sending mixed signals, spend time with God confessing your need for repentance. Then don't be afraid of honesty with your children. God will use it to help your children understand that honesty before God makes all things go better.

Time to Pray

1. Thank God for His salvation in your life using Ps. 118:21.

   _____

   _____

   _____

2. What does Ps. 40:10 urge you to do? How does it apply to your children?

   _____

   _____

   _____

3. Ask God to keep you focused on how He sought, found, and rescued you.

   _____

   _____

   _____

4. Ask God to show you how He is actively pursuing your children. Record the signs:

   _____

   _____

   _____

Other Ways to Share the Salvation Story

When Jesus wanted to share how precious salvation is, He used object lessons. He talked about treasure, planting seeds, a lost coin. He talked about things that people understood. We should follow His example. There are two object lessons in the

Christian Church that can help parents explain salvation. Christian baptism and the Lord's Supper are both very visible metaphors. Make sure you sit with young children during these special times. Encourage them to ask questions. Answer them in ways that retell the story of salvation. Talk about how you're praying that they'll make a personal decision to follow Christ.

Let the Sacraments Teach

- Make sure your children attend baptism and communion services.

- Sit with them and model interest and reverence.

- Talk about the baptism testimonies of new Christians.

- Encourage questions.

- Look for signs that they're connecting God's love with Jesus' death.

- Use their questions as opportunities to tell the salvation story.

- Watch for evidences that your children understand more with each new experience.

- When your children demonstrate a personal understanding, talk about when they might participate in Christian baptism or receiving the Lord's Supper.

Easter Reviews the Story

Easter is another time to rehearse the salvation story. No matter what your family traditions include, make sure your priority is to treat Good Friday and Easter more as *holy* days than as *holi*days. There are lots of ways to do this. Some will fit your family better than others. The important thing is to choose special ways to help everyone remember and understand what Jesus did for us.

Ideas for Making Easter Special

- Plant a seed that will show a green shoot by Easter. Talk about how this tells the story of Jesus dying and coming back to life.
- Take a walk with young children at Easter time. Look for signs of new life. Use them as reminders of the way God makes our lives new when we live for Him.
- Hide Easter symbols around the house: a cross, a lamb, bread, a long nail, a stone, thorns, a bag of 30 coins. When a family member finds a symbol, have him or her bring it to a family meal and talk about its meaning.
- Buy or make pretzels. A Catholic monk twisted leftover bread dough to look like people praying with arms crossed over their chests. Talk about ways your family could be praying during Easter.
- Attend a Good Friday service.
- Watch the children's *JESUS* film together, and talk about it.
- On the Saturday before Easter, eat the family meal by candlelight. Talk about how the disciples must have felt after Jesus was crucified. Keep lights low the rest of the night to remember how sad and scared the disciples must have been.
- Talk about the Early Church's practice of greeting Christians with "Jesus is risen," and the response "He is risen indeed." See who will say it first on Easter morning. Encourage family members to say it many times beyond Easter.

If salvation is God's number-one priority for our sons and daughters, we should spend priority time praying about this key decision in their lives. Praying for their salvation helps us participate in God's eternal purpose for them. The problem is that many parents don't know how to pray for salvation. In my parenting journey, I learned that a prayer for my daughter's salvation included some key prayers for me. I learned that praying about salvation isn't a formula—it's a lifestyle. It's a prayer that keeps me tuned to God's eternal priorities for my daughter. After all, parenting isn't about getting our kids through school or getting them married; it's about getting them to heaven.

How to Pray for Your Child's Salvation

1. Tune your heart to the longing of God's heart for your child.

No matter how much love and good intentions we have for our children, they're no match for the perfect and eternal love of God. His is a reaching love, a patient love, a merciful love. As parents, we become God's most valuable intercessors for the child He lends us while we're on earth. The more we connect to God's love for our children, the more sensitive we become to our need to reflect His love in all our parenting.

Rewrite the following verses, inserting your child's name into them. Use them as your prayer guides.

Luke 19:10: _____

_____

_____

1 Tim. 2:3-4: _____

_____

_____

Sam. 23:5: _____

_____

_____

1 Thess. 5:9: _____

_____

_____

God makes it undeniably clear that He has provided everything necessary to bring salvation to our children. Nothing is missing. He celebrates every decision to accept the gift of salvation. The more we focus on the intensity of God's longing for our children, the more we realize how infinitely more God works for the salvation of our children than anything we do. We understand our place as God's representatives to model God's heart to them. That sends me to my knees with my own shortcomings. Before I can pray for my child, I need to pray for myself.

There's another advantage for focusing on God's love before focusing on ours. It's God's love in us that enables a better relationship with our children. This is especially critical if you're dealing with a child's rebellion or rejection.

2. Understand that God will use your children's strengths and needs to bring your children to himself.

I was desperately praying for the salvation of someone very important to me. I found myself praying with great fear and anxiety, because I knew how critical the decision for salvation was becoming. I looked at the decisions and life issues of this person and saw only what was taking her away from God. I wanted God to take away the things she was doing that provided increased risks and continued to separate her from God. But nothing seemed to change.

It was in a Bible study that someone taught me that God draws people to himself using their strengths, not their weaknesses. I changed my prayer focus and began asking God to use specific strengths to get her attention. That's when I began to recognize where God *was* at work in her life. My prayers changed from prayers that were paralyzed by fear to prayers that saw more specific ways to cooperate with God's plan of search and rescue.

Paul's conversion story illustrates this truth in a bold way. God brought Paul to his knees in the middle of his fanatical pursuit of Christians. He was an in-your-face guy who needed an in-your-face, life-stopping revelation from God. As we think of Paul before conversion, he was single-minded, outspoken, courageous, a magnetic leader, and strong-willed. I'm sure that there were a lot of Christians who prayed that God would take some of Saul's strengths away. If Saul couldn't use his strengths against the Christians, they would be better off. Instead, God drew Saul to Him through his strengths to claim those strengths for His purposes. After conversion, Paul's basic characteristics or personality didn't change. Rather, they were forcefully channeled in a different way.

List the strengths of each of your children. _____

_____

_____

_____

How could these strengths lead your children to God? _____

_____

_____

_____

How could this change your prayer focus? _____

_____

_____

_____

---

3. Reject *don't-let* prayers and learn to pray *for* your child.

Prayer is a positive activity. It's a communication channel that connects to a God who desires to say yes more than no. For that reason, pray *for* your children. Pray *for* God to use their strengths to bring an awareness of their need for salvation. Pray *for* them to look to God for answers to difficult situations. Pray *for* a deepening awareness of God's love.

Fear pushes us to pray *don't-let* prayers. *Don't let* a friend persuade in wrong ways. *Don't let* my son lose his job and get discouraged. *Don't let* my daughter get frustrated with her singleness. Many times, *don't-let* prayers focus on things that aren't happening. Praying *for* our children acknowledges realities and asks God to use those realities to help our children recognize His love and work in their lives.

Praying *for* our children requires that we see them as God sees them. This becomes crucial for a child who rejects God. It's even more critical for a child who rejects a parent in the process of rejecting God. It's then that a parent can feel some of the pain that God feels when one of His children rejects Him. Just think of it: rejection never affects the quality, patience, or endurance of God's love. God's model of unconditional love can enable us to see our children through His love instead of our hurt. It helps us to pray *for* them.

Praying *for* Our Children

Write your children's names in the following scriptures and use them to pray *for* the salvation of your children.

1 Cor. 2:9 _____

_____

Heb. 10:22 _____

_____

John 5:24 _____

_____

Isa. 55:7 _____

_____

1 John 1:9 _____

_____

Heavenly Father,

We praise you for your faithfulness to us. We thank you for the gift of our children. They have blessed our hearts and bring great joy to us. We are reminded, however, that you have entrusted them to our care and nourishment. Help us as parents reflect your love in all of our actions. May they see Jesus Christ through our lives. Above all, we pray that they will put their faith and trust in Jesus as their personal Savior and Lord. Keep them in your love; direct their lives as they grow in faith. Protect them from all that would harm, and meet every true need. May they become committed followers of Jesus Christ, joining the family circle that has no end.

We pray in the name of your Son.

Amen.

Dave and Becky Le Shana

Praying for Prodigals

Few challenges in a parent's life bring more pain than when a child rejects God and chooses values, friendships, and activities that do not please God. However, it's also true that when a child is away from God, it's a time when that child, no matter his or her age, needs the persistent, faith-sourced, intercessory prayer of a parent. How do you pray *for* a wayward child when everything in your heart wants to pray *against* wrong choices, *against* bad influences, *against* activities that take him or her farther away? How do you pray with the passion that you feel without letting that passion degenerate into desperate responses? While there's no guaranteed formula for helping a child find his or her way back to God's heart, perhaps the following principles and focus priorities will help.

1. Don't play games about your children's spiritual condition.

"She's a *good* girl," her mother said. "She just made a bad choice." She was right to a point. Her daughter had made a bad choice. That's what sin is. It chooses an action or attitude that

God has said is wrong. When my husband wanted to talk to her about her daughter's need for repentance, the mother bristled. She could not face the truth about her daughter's spiritual condition. Instead of becoming an intercessor, she became an enabler.

Don't be afraid to call your children lost. Don't water down the problem of sin. It's another area in which God deals with realities, even when we won't. If Jesus wouldn't let the religious leaders of His day play word games to defend their traditional spirituality, we shouldn't either. We should look for the fruit of a transformed heart. It's not about expecting a level of maturity that's not age-appropriate. It's about looking for the signs that a child wants to obey God.

---

*The knowledge of sin is the
beginning of salvation.*
—Epicurus

---

2. Find out where God is already working in your child's life, and focus your prayers there.

The fact that God is making you aware of your need to pray for your children's salvation is one way you cooperate with His work. Don't get ahead of God. Sometimes it requires asking Him to show you where He's working, because it may be difficult to see. Look for the places God is making your son or daughter more sensitive to spiritual things. Pray for a softened heart in your child, and look for that softening. Consider it an opening, and enter there. Read scriptures about salvation. Look at the variety of ways God worked in different Bible characters. Talk to a Christian whose life parallels your child's detour. Find out what made a difference and what created obstacles. You can say too much too soon or at the wrong time or get in an argument and do more damage than good. Ask God to protect you from saying or doing anything that gives your child a reason to reject God's invitation again.

How Can I Start Praying Specifically?

Use the following questions to identify a prayer list:
Where is God making my child more sensitive to Him?
What questions is my child asking about God or life?
Where is my child open to my prayers?
What circumstance could God use as an open door?
What captures my child's attention? How could God use it?

My Prayer List for

_____

1.

2.

3.

4.

5.

3. Ask God to help you match the words of your prayers to the actions of your life.

Nothing speaks more directly to your child than how you live your life for God in the middle of your daily routine. It's the life they see, not the words you say, that makes the biggest difference. You are a living Bible, especially if your children see no need to read it on their own. Practice the spiritual graces of confession, forgiveness, kindness, long-suffering, and self-control. Remember that they live in your life to the degree you allow God's Holy Spirit to be in charge. Demonstrate your value of godly priorities in areas of leisure, work, and relationships. Pray daily the heart-purifying prayer "See if there be any offensive way in *me*" (Ps. 139:24, emphasis added). The stakes are high. Your obedience and daily growth in Christ are absolutely critical if you want your child to see that salvation makes a meaningful difference in life.

Remember: it's not about living a perfect life before your kids. Sometimes it's the way you handle wrong responses that speak the loudest. Take responsibility for wrong attitudes and actions. Don't blame others or even a difficult situation. Ask forgiveness directly and specifically if you blow it. Don't apologize for being a work in progress. Your children need to know how to handle the same things.

4. Give God your fear about what might happen if your child continues to say no to God.

Fear of *what might happen* paralyzes. W*hat if* fears aren't reality. Remember: God deals with realities. Many times it's the lack of control you feel about the eternal destiny of your child that overwhelms you. Acknowledge your feelings of helplessness before God. Then acknowledge God's all-seeing power. He'll meet you at the point of your fear to help you address it so that you don't respond to your child out of fear. Always allow God to show you how much He loves your child. You can't say or pray anything that will make God act with more love for your child than He already has. Let God's perfect love for your son or daughter and you drive out fear and give you hope.

Perfect love drives out fear.

—1 John 4:18

5. Remember that you are only one part of God's search-and-rescue team for your child.

Listen to the salvation stories of people around you. You'll be amazed at the large search-and-rescue team God has for His lost children. While Christian parents are definitely part of the team, they often are not the ones to make that last critical connection. Pray for the search-and-rescue team God has raised up or wants to raise up for your child. Don't carry the whole burden. Find a prayer partner. Understand that your child's salvation is not your responsibility—it is God's. Your responsibility is to "live such good lives . . . [that your child] may see your good deeds and glorify God" (1 Pet. 2:12).

6. Pray to release your child to God's complete control.

You cannot control your child into salvation. It's a love work of God. He whispers. He invites. He confronts in love. He speaks the truth. He always watches and waits. He always loves. He'll always forgive. Develop those characteristics in your reaching love for a child away from God. Since God is the author and full embodiment of each of those characteristics, could you release your child to anyone more capable of drawing your child to God? Pray with that confident understanding.

7. Ask God to make your child *heart sick.*

It was Pascal who said, "There is a God-shaped vacuum in every heart." Nothing fills that space besides God. It's the place where God wants to live. When He doesn't live in our sons and daughters, He can't meet those longings in ways that securely satisfy. Restless activities expressed as rebellion, rejection, and experimentation all point to this kind of heartsickness. If your son or daughter still lives at home, it's especially easy to give priority prayer time to the actions of sin rather than the heart problem. Find a balance here. Pray that your child feels his or her heartsickness and becomes open to the only effective treatment plan: salvation.

There is a God-shaped vacuum in every heart.

—*Pascal*

---

8. Pray that your child will desire the benefits of salvation.

Why anyone would want to reject God's offer of perfect love, never-failing relationship, and eternal provisions makes no sense. But some people do. We lay it at the feet of dysfunctional families, peer pressure, secular influences, genetic bents, and a list of other symptoms. However, a sinful lifestyle is the result of choosing sin and self-centeredness over God. But why? What picture of salvation are they rejecting? Do they really see the benefits of turning toward God? Review the benefit for yourself to make sure your life reflects them. Then pray that your child begins to see the benefits for his or her own life.

What are the benefits of salvation? Use the following scriptures to start your list. Pray through them daily for a week. Ask God to reveal anything in your own life that doesn't allow these benefits to show through.

Ps. 119:41 _____

Rom. 6:23 _____

Rom. 8:31-32 _____

Rom. 10:11 _____

2 Cor. 1:20 _____

Do you begin to see what you're asking God to communicate to your child? Salvation shares a never-failing love in a society where human relationships often fail. Salvation alone gives eternal life in a world where nothing else lasts forever. Salvation proves how God is on our side so that nothing we do out of obedience to Him brings shame. These are exciting things to pray about.

9. Find a prayer partner.

Not only do you need someone who shares your intercessory vigil for your son or daughter—you need a prayer partner who will make you accountable for your actions and responses. It can be another parent who has a prodigal child. Or it can be a person whose spiritual maturity and discernment you need as you pray for your child. Check in with each other weekly, if possible, or at least monthly. Give your prayer partner permission to ask three questions: How have you been praying for your child? What answers, lessons, or direction are you sensing from God? What have you done to strengthen your relationship with your child? Always do more praying than talking. That's what a *prayer* partner is.

Accountability Questions

How have you been praying for your child?

What answers, lessons, or direction are you sensing from God?

What have you done to strengthen your relationship with your child?

Pray About It

Is there anything in your life story that helps you understand your child's life choices that do not embrace God?

_____

_____

_____

_____

What responses from other people helped or hindered your path to God? _____

_____

_____

_____

Review Luke's story of the prodigal child (Luke 15:11-32). What part speaks directly to your experience as the parent of a prodigal? _____

_____

_____

Praying the Prayer God Longs to Answer

Praying for the salvation of our children is the prayer that God longs to answer. Do we really understand that there's nothing, absolutely nothing, that God wants more for our children than for them to be safely welcomed into His family? Understanding this should enable us to pray with a freedom and boldness that's not self-manufactured. This kind of prayer must be completely rooted in who God is, that mysterious and inexplicable balance between love and justice, permission and discipline, grace and judgment. It's a prayer that brings God's perspective with it, a perspective we can see as soon as we let go of anything that shouts "My way!" The prayer that God will answer reflects His true character in all ways. It confirms scripture without exception. It corrects life priorities, values, and direction without apology.

Let us begin, as never before, to pray for our children. Pray not only because we love them but also because God longs for them. He gives us the honor of being the channels through whom His blessing is brought down.

—Andrew Murray, *Teach Me to Pray*

Persistent Prayer

Whether you're praying for young children to make their first profession of faith or praying that a child will come back to God in repentance, always pray knowing that you're praying the prayer that God longs to answer. Don't ever stop praying it. Persistent prayer doesn't make God love you or your child any more than He already does. Instead, it keeps you available as God's instrument in the life of one or more of His children. Pray when you don't see any results. Pray harder when you do. Don't ever give up praying. As long as your child is able to choose, there's time to choose God.

More Scriptures to Pray

*I wait for your salvation, O LORD,
and I follow your commands.*
—Ps. 119:166

It is good to wait quietly for the salvation of the LORD.
—Lam. 3:26

*He who sacrifices thank offerings honors me, and he pre-
pares the way so that I may show him the salvation of God*
—Ps. 50:23

*My soul faints with longing for your salvation,
but I have put my hope in your word.*
—Ps. 119:81

*In the same way, the Spirit helps us in our weakness.
We do not know what we ought to pray for,
but the Spirit himself intercedes for us
with groans that words cannot express.*
—Rom. 8:26

*Pray for us, too, that God may open a door for our message,
so that we may proclaim the mystery of Christ, for which I
am in chains. Pray that I may proclaim it clearly, as I should.*
—Col. 4:3-4

*Pray also for me, that whenever I open my mouth,
words may be given me so that I will fearlessly
make known the mystery of the gospel.*
—Eph. 6:19

*Whatever happens, conduct yourselves in a
manner worthy of the gospel of Christ.*
—Phil. 1:27

Your Turn

- Pray that your child develops a hunger and thirst for righteousness (Matt. 5:6). What about your life demonstrates the hunger and thirst that you're praying for in your child?
- Pray that your child understands how God and His way will meet his or her needs in ways that no other person or pursuit can. How does Phil. 4:19 describe this filling?
- Pray that the eyes of your child's heart will be opened to God.
- According to Eph. 1:18-21, what might your child see with these heart-eyes?
- Using principles and key scriptures from this chapter, write a prayer for your child's salvation.

Praying for Your Child's Salvation

1. Pray for the spiritual health of your child *first*.
2. Review the meaning of salvation, and pray that God will help you live it daily.
3. Pray for opportunities to share and review God's salvation story.
4. Pray that God will use your child's strengths to bring about salvation.
5. Be willing to accurately assess your child's spiritual condition.
6. Never stop praying.

He will bring you a message through which you and all your household will be saved.

—Acts 11:14

My Prayer

God,

He's in between friends, and I feel his limbo. There's lostness in his eyes that I don't know how to address. I fear he'll reach out too fast to fill his loneliness the wrong way. If I only knew what was coming next, I could help him wait. How can I encourage patience for this transition without a map?

In Between

Dear In Between,

I am the beginning and the end. I am already in between. I can lead you both.

Your Guide

4
Praying Through Transitions

*People are most receptive to God
when they are . . . in transition.*
—Rick Warren, *The Purpose-Driven Life*

Transitions are processes for turning corners. They mark changes between growth stages, between life events, between relationships—between anything. That's what makes them frustrating: they're in between. There's a sense of ending and beginning all at once. Unless it's very clear what's next, the tendency is to hold on to the familiar or rush too quickly into something new. Either can make our children miss the next healthy step.

While transition times can be very frustrating, they're also very important. Do you remember what your high school English teacher taught you about transitions? They help you to go from one idea to the next by connecting what went before with what's to come. I call them bridges. They connect the known with the unknown.

Transition . . .

The process of passing from one form, state, or stage to another: change, passage, shift, transit.
    —*Roget's II: The New Thesaurus,* Third Edition, 1995

Maturity and development depend on going from the known to the unknown. Unfortunately, our children can struggle when they feel stuck in between. It can seem as if nothing's happening—a time of limbo, a time of emptiness.

But something *is* happening. Transitions are key times. They're all about moving forward, not stalling. What our children do with them influences what comes next. That's why prayer is needed during transitions.

Our children experience transitions every time they go through another developmental stage. Every summer is a transition. So is the time between friendships, dating relationships, or jobs. Transition is the bridge that prepares for change. Something has ended; something new is on the way.

Key Transitions

Below are examples of transitions in our children's growth. Can you name others?

Physical

crawler to walker _____

child to adolescent _____

adolescent to young adult _____

Mental/emotional

literal to conceptual _____

dependent to independent _____

self-centered to others-centered _____

Educational

home to kindergarten _____

elementary to middle _____

high school to college _____

Spiritual

knowing about God to

   knowing God _____

reciting prayers to
  talking to God _____

knowing Bible truth to
  applying Bible lessons _____

Balancing in Between

Have you ever tried to step from a stable dock into a rocking boat? It can be a treacherous, balance-robbing experience. As your brain processes the moving object in front of you, everything inside tells you to not step onto the unsteady surface. You do it anyway because you want to take a boat ride. Carefully, your foot finds the bobbing boat. But here's the trick: the longer you keep one foot on the secure, familiar dock and one foot on the rocking boat, the more precarious your "transition." At some point, you must stop dividing your weight between the two surfaces. Knowing how to do that—and when—is the difference between taking a boat ride and going for a swim. There is a completely different world to see beyond the dock, but you must put both feet into the boat to experience it.

> In what ways does this boat-dock illustration remind me of a transition in my child's life?

Some transitions last longer than others. That can challenge endurance, patience, and a positive outlook. The longer the transition, the bigger the challenge. However, long transitions provide more time to learn something new. Think of some of the transitions Bible characters endured.

Moses learned about wilderness survival and herding flocks during his 40-year transition. These would become critical lessons when God called him to lead a nation through the wilderness. The children of Israel had their own 40-year wilderness

---

What did the following people learn during transition?

- **Moses (Exod. 2:15—3:1)** *after* leaving his childhood Egypt and *before* returning as God's spokesman. _____

  _____

  _____

- **The children of Israel (Deut. 1:1-3; 28:2, 15, 62)** *after* the Red Sea miracle and *before* entering the Promised Land.

  _____

  _____

- **David (1 Sam. 16:13; 17:50; 18:14; 30:6; 2 Sam. 2:4)** *after* Samuel anointed him as the next king and *before* he was crowned king. _____

  _____

---

transition. They needed to learn that obedience is nonnegotiable with God. Because they didn't learn that lesson quickly, their transition was longer than necessary. And then there was David. David lived with the knowledge that he would be king. There were many years between Samuel's anointing him as the king God had chosen and the time when he actually wore the crown. Skimming through the chapters of David's story reveals how he learned to hear and obey God's voice as he confronted the giant and other enemies—no small transitional lessons.

Don't underestimate lessons learned in transition!

Why pray during times of transition?

There are three key reasons we should use transitions as times to pray for our children.

1. Transitions prepare us for change.

Change either excites or scares us. For certain, change gives us items for our prayer lists. We pray because we don't want our children to stumble into the next growth stage or life event without knowing what they need to know. Unfortunately, we can't prepare them for everything. That's why we pray. God sees the future and waits to use obedience as raw material for the good things He wants to bring in and through change. God needs our obedience as well as our children's, especially if children are at home. If we give God a chance to work in us parents, He can protect us from responses that will not help our children during transition. It simply reminds us that as we pray for our children, we must pray for ourselves. Whatever change is on the horizon for our children changes something for us too. We need to be ready for changes that we can't control. Only God can help us do that.

> *Dear Father,*
>
> *It's hard to believe we're leaving our son at college today. It seems like yesterday that we were leaving him at preschool. All he needed then for security was a sack lunch, his favorite baseball cap, Pooh Bear, and his mother's hug. Today it takes three trunks of clothes, a computer, a CD player with speakers, a tennis racquet, twelve pairs of shoes, posters from groups we never have to hear again, and the one thing that hasn't changed in the last 19 years: his mother's hug.*
>
> *We find ourselves praying the same prayer we prayed the night our blue-eyed, blond-haired, eight-pound-six-ounce boy was born—"O Lord, what do we do now?" You took our apprehension and fear of the unknown that night and have guided us as a family. Tonight we say good-bye to our six-foot, blond-haired (for now!) handsome, young man. We pray that he'll always be true to you, for you've always been faithful to him.*
>
> > *With a heart full of hope and memories,*
> > *A surrendering father*
> > *Gary Sivewright*

2. Transitions give time for evaluation.

Time is the most important gift of transitions. They give time to think about what has happened. They give time to grieve what may have been lost. They give time to heal. As we pray for our children in transition, we pray they'll understand their context from God's perspective. We pray they'll take time to identify and apply the right lessons from a past experience. We pray that a time of transition won't discourage them.

The heart of these prayers is to acknowledge truth. If we believe John 8:32, which says, "The truth will set you free," then we'll do whatever it takes to help our children identity and accept truth. However, we must understand that truth goes beyond perception. My father-in-law was known for saying "The truth's the truth." It was his way of saying that it didn't matter how you felt about something or whether you had a different opinion—truth changes for no one. Our children will not learn to look for truth as a natural reflex. As parents, we must model how to look for God's truth. That means we have to pray for the willingness to face any truth about ourselves or our children. Transitions give us time to reflect, evaluate, and discuss these things.

Transition Time Ideas

For Children Living at Home
1. Invite your child to accompany you on an errand. Talk about feelings, frustrations, and future possibilities.
2. Take your child out for an afternoon or evening treat. Ask questions to stimulate talking. Answer questions, and save advice for another time.
3. Make a list with your child to identify how to creatively use a transition time.
4. Put together a transition basket. Fill it with encouraging notes, something fun, a book that deals with the transition circumstance, a special treat, a coupon.
5. Is there a special project the two of you would enjoy doing? Transition gives time for such activities.
6. Plant a seed, and see how many days it takes before something visible changes. Talk about the implications.

For Adult Children Not Living at Home
1. Call or send notes more often.
2. Send a phone card, gift card, or restaurant coupon, and encourage your child to use it with an encouraging friend.
3. Send a "transition" plant with a message to watch how slowly plants change before flowering.
4. Send a "care package." Include things to make your son or daughter laugh, think, and act.
5. Share a transition story from your own life. Be specific about whether you handled the time wisely or not. Share how you applied the transition lesson.

3. Transitions give time to *con*fess and *add*ress, before making *prog*ress.

Confess

Some of the most difficult transitions are the consequences of sinful decisions. During these kinds of transitions, we pray that our children will learn how important confessing sin is. James 5:16 reminds us to "confess your sins to each other and pray for each other so that you may be healed." It's important for children, no matter their ages, to learn that confession frees, while keeping secrets, protecting lies, or defending sinful choices enslaves. To confess simply means to accept God's perspective on an attitude or action. It involves acknowledging this to God and to anyone else involved. Confession also accepts God's prescription for sin: forgiveness and repentance. Be careful about using any other name for sin. It prevents the healing that comes from forgiveness.

Address

It's impossible to skip confession and try to *address* important lessons. When we do, the process deteriorates into self-help. Confession refocuses the heart to want God's way. How can someone want God's way before accepting God's evaluation? The lessons that will make a difference make more sense after agreeing with God's judgment about actions or attitudes.

Progress

Confession clears the way for progress. Applying key lessons makes way for the growth goals that will mean progress. As your child acts on new lessons and new discoveries, look for changes. Point out the difference it makes. Help your child mark the tiny steps of progress. Affirm each new try in the same way you coached first steps.

Encouraging Confession

- Develop a relationship that encourages your children to confess anything.
- Accept a confession without lecturing.
- Immediately lead your child to ask God for forgiveness.
- Practice open communication within your family. Confession won't occur when family members don't communicate with each other.
- Understand that learning to confess to parents is a crucial first step in learning to confess to God.
- Recognize your role as God's representative to accept confession with forgiveness. Respond to your child's confession as God's representative.
- Encourage your children to find a prayer/accountability partner, especially when they become teenagers and young adults.
- Model confession. When you've reacted too quickly or hurt your child with words or an attitude, confess it aloud, and ask your child's forgiveness.

Transition Is a Gift

As I've shared with parents, I've learned that prayer requests for our children usually heighten when something is wrong or hard or confusing. Many times parents and children struggle with transitional issues that come from time factors. While it may feel as if time is a part of the problem, it may be part of the answer. As parents, we can see transition as the helpful time that it is. We can pray for the gifts transitions offer. That will allow us to feel less fear during these in-between times, and transitions can do their good work in us and our children.

Adolescence is a border between childhood and adulthood. Like all borders, it's teeming with energy and fraught with danger.

—Mary Pipher, 20th-century psychologist

Adolescence: A Critical Transition

We only *think* we understand what helplessness is as we carry a newborn in our arms. Whatever our definition of helplessness is during that first week of parenthood, it's nothing compared to the helpless feelings we'll experience as we parent a teenager. No matter how many books we read, we're never ready for their push for independence and the tug-of-war this time introduces. While they're changing physically and emotionally, our lives aren't behaving in predictable ways either. It's a stage that tests every parenting skill we possess. Sometimes we wonder who needs prayer more, our teenager or ourselves.

Of course, the answer is that we *both* need prayer. We can take ourselves to God first. We can admit our insecurities and hurt feelings when we're left out of their lives. We can allow God to meet those needs so that we'll be ready to listen to God's instructions about how to pray for our teenagers.

A Wordless Prayer
    She came home hurting today. I knew the moment she walked in the door that something was very wrong. A heaviness . . . a deep sadness seemed to envelope her spirit as she sat at the kitchen table, head in her hands. When I asked what was wrong, she refused to say anything, other than "I had a bad day. I don't want to talk about it."

Not knowing what else to do, I stepped behind her chair and began to gently rub her shoulders and back. As I did, I watched a lone tear slip from the corner of her eye and etch a quiet path down her cheek. Oh, how this mother's heart ached for her daughter!

—*Bette Dale Moore*

As you pray for your teenager—

1. Ask God to help you connect to your teen's feelings before you connect to the problem.

God wants to deal with real needs in the life of your teen. If your teen feels overwhelmed by peer pressure because of insecurity or acts out anger because of hurt, God will meet that teen at the abyss of need before He deals with behavior. Make sure you do too. Give your teenager a chance to voice feelings about an action, circumstance, or person without passing judgment on those feelings.

What can you do or stop doing to encourage your teenager to share feelings with you?

_____

_____

2. Ask God to show you how to connect with your teen without using words.

Teenagers stop hearing words. The mother in the illustration used a shoulder massage to communicate her concern. What can you do? Squeeze a hand? Shoot baskets? Share a soda? Or maybe it's just the way your eyes deliver a message of love. God will give you ideas if you let Him. Practice many kinds of wordless messages every day. They will encourage your teenager to talk with you in time.

Make a list of wordless ways that could help you connect to your teen:

_____   _____

_____   _____

_____   _____

_____   _____

3. Remind yourself often that God knows what you don't know.

God will never hold you responsible for what you can't know —only for what you can. If you refuse to see the truth God wants you to see, then you can't participate in the answer God wants to give. His answer always finds its foundation in truth and reality. Pray often that you'll be willing to know anything God wants you to know about your teenager so that the two of you are working on the same side to bring your teen through these difficult direction-setting days.

Lord,

Why must growing up be so difficult? When she was seven, it was much easier. When something hurt, she told me what had happened and where the pain was. I anointed the injury with medicine and Band-Aids, held her tight, and kissed it all better. But now that she's 17, she often seems to hold her pain inside and pushes me away when I try to help.

O my loving Father, I know she's your daughter too. You know her far better than I do, for you created her and knit her together in my womb. You brought her into this world, and you walk with her through every step of every day.

Help me to know how to comfort her when she hurts. Give me the wisdom to know when to probe and push on her wounds and when to simply step back and love—perhaps through a touch, perhaps through a look, perhaps

> *through a prayer. Quiet her heart. Ease her pain. Let her*
> *know that her mom loves her, that her dad loves her, and*
> *most of all that her Heavenly Father loves her.*
> > *With great love,*
> > *Her mother*
> > *Bette Dale Moore*

God has been preparing you for this time. Parenting your teenager will take all the skills God has been developing in you. Whatever you need, whether it is patience, flexibility, or discernment, God has it ready for you in rich supply. Knowing you have these needs should make you more willing to present your vulnerabilities to God and ask for His help. Remember: He's done this before.

Praying for Your Teenager

- Thank God that adolescence is a normal stage of development, and pray Ps. 139:13-16 with this in mind.
- Put your children's names in Titus 3:13 and your name in verse 14 as you ask God to help you sense the true needs of your teenager.
- Pray Eph. 4:29 and make a list of the ways you affirm your teenager with *and* without words.
- Pray that God's Spirit rests on you and your teenager in the specific ways listed in Isa. 11:2-3.

Whether transition is a normal break between life stages or an unwelcome break from illness, accident, or divorce, transition is a critical time. God wants to use transition to help your child review and refocus. That gives you an important prayer list. Use the following to help you focus your prayers in growth-producing ways. Look for the ways God answers these prayers, and see how they become a part of bringing about even bigger answers.

How do I pray for my child in transition?

1. Pray that your child will use the transition to learn from the past.

What lessons does God want your child to learn about His faithfulness, leadership, mercy, will, or love? How will those lessons help in the next stage of life? Pray that these lessons will surface and your child will recognize them. Then pray that your child will apply the lessons.

2. Pray that you and your child will treat transition as something productive.

Whether your child is between jobs or between living at home and moving out, transition is not limbo. There is always something to do. Transition sometimes sets its own agenda. Moving requires packing. Surgery requires healing. Death—even the death of dreams—requires grieving. Even when nothing overtly changes, it should be a time for internal strengthening and change. Pray Eph. 1:18. Pray that your child will fill the transition with actions and attitudes that will help him or her be ready for the next life event.

Helping Your Child Transition

1. Talk about what has ended, especially feelings about it.
2. Ask your child to identify lessons.
3. Encourage your child to focus forward, not backward.
4. Brainstorm possibilities for the future as well as for the transition.
5. Explore ways to improve a skill necessary for a new beginning.
6. Encourage choices that make a positive difference.
7. Celebrate whatever ends the transition.
8. Talk about God's timing and faithfulness during the transition.

3. Pray that perfect love will cast out fear.

It's common to fear what we don't know. However, 1 John 4:18 announces that "There is no fear in love. But perfect love drives out fear." Instead of praying against fear, pray that God's perfect love will fill, calm, and steady your child. Pray that His love will fill you. Pray that your child comes to understand that God is involved in every detail and wants His plan only to protect, fulfill, and complete your child. In your prayer, thank God for the evidence of His love in your child's life. The more you focus on God's love, the less room there will be for fear.

> Father,
>   He became a teenager today. You know all the fears he has and I have. Thank you, Lord, that you're our guide through these passages. May both he and I always remember your ways. Strengthen him against the pressures that will come and the temptations that stalk a teenager. Build your spirit into his life. Train his conscience to respond to your ways, and nurture his heart in the ways of righteousness. Keep him pure for your service, and give him fruitful and meaningful teen years. I offer this prayer in the strong name of Jesus.
>
>   With hope,
>   Trusting father
>   C. Neil Strait

When You Pray Through Transitions . . .

1. God's plan prepares your child for this transition.

God has planted the seeds of whatever your child needs to endure a difficult or confusing transition. You get to water those seeds. Nurture the smallest signs of hope, perseverance, creativity, obedience, or other characteristics that God wants to grow in your child during a time of change. Never forget that God's will for your child is that goodness and mercy will follow him or her all the days of his or her life and that your child will dwell in God's house forever (Ps. 23:6).

2. Pray that your child will identify a relationship, a lesson, a skill, or a strength that will be important in the next stage of growth.

This helps transition face forward and not backward. It places an element of control back into a time that might feel out of control. It helps your child feel productive. Be careful not to push too hard or move too quickly. Offer suggestions, but allow your child to make the choice. Celebrate discoveries and new opportunities in ways that fit the achievement. Ps. 119:173 is a good prayer to pray as you desire God to be the most important helping hand your child receives.

> What relationship, lesson, skill, or spiritual fruit will help your child get ready for the next step of growth? Write your prayer based on Phil. 1:6
>
> _____
>
> _____
>
> _____
>
> _____
>
> _____
>
> _____
>
> _____

3. Look for predictable stages in transition.

Some transitions have fairly predictable stages. The journey through grief takes one through stages of denial, anger, and resolution. Summer vacation and the school year can be marked off by the calendar. The transition into a new job starts with the adrenaline rush of a new learning curve followed by settling into a routine. Doctors tell us what to expect when healing from surgery or a broken bone. Think about predictable stages to the transition your child faces. Even if your child doesn't want to talk about the stages, you can pray during them. Recognizing the stages can help mark progress even when it feels as if nothing much is happening.

4. Pray that your child will recognize the dangers of staying in a transition too long.

A teenager or young adult sometimes hangs onto a relationship because it's comfortable. A high school graduate may cling to the first full-time job and postpone college. There are many reasons that people stay in transition too long. Pray that your child is willing to accept an end to something comfortable in order to make way for a growth-stimulating step. Pray that he or she will lean on God for security in a time when being in between feels insecure. Pray Phil. 1:9 every day for a child who seems stuck in transition unnecessarily. In discussing your concerns with your child, learn to lead with affirmation rather than criticism or a lecture. Affirm God-given personality traits. Affirm your child's desire to follow God's will. Affirm God's desire to lead. Always make it a time of nurture.

Write your Phil. 1:9 prayer here:

_____

_____

_____

_____

_____

_____

_____

_____

_____

_____

5. Pray that your child's transition will mean transitional growth for you as well.

No matter how much you prepare for the expected transitions from home to kindergarten or from childhood to adolescence, your child's transition also means transition for you. Pray for yourself. Pray that the transition will help you learn self-control, patience, endurance, and faith in very specific, growth-producing ways. Don't expect growth from your child that you can't address in your own life.

Pray a Gal. 5:22 prayer for yourself during this transition:

_____

_____

_____

_____

_____

_____

_____

_____

_____

Transition Is About Time

When Lisa finished high school, we all took a deep breath. It had been a long, hard, incredible push. We were all ready for a rest and a party! It was what followed that was unpredictably difficult. We had worked so hard helping Lisa achieve her goal to graduate from high school that we did not effectively address her next life goal. Because of Lisa's unique set of disabilities coupled with the limited resources of our community, getting a job became as difficult as crossing the Red Sea. It forced all of us into an unwanted transition. I knew that it was a time when Lisa could easily lose heart. In fact, she nearly did. I recognized it as a time when I needed to be in prayer for her. It would be easy to lose everything we had gained if she gave up too soon. I had to do something, so I prayed.

I prayed for creative ways to fill the transition time. I prayed for Lisa's endurance as well as mine. I prayed that we would learn ways to support each other. I prayed for the Red Sea to open.

Praying Through Transition

1. Pray that God will make you and your child ready for change and growth (1 Pet. 1:13).

2. Pray that you and your child will use transition to evaluate attitudes and actions from God's perspective (Phil. 4:8).

3. Pray that your child will use the confess-address-progress strategy. Make it a family model (James 5:16; Col. 1:10-12; James 1:4).

4. Pray that God will help you connect with your child's feelings about transition (Col. 2:2).

5. Ask God to help you find wordless ways to encourage your child.

6. Pray that your child will learn important lessons from the past to build a bridge to the future (2 Tim. 3:14; Eph. 4:15).

7. Pray that perfect love will cast out fear in your child and in you (1 John 4:18).

The good news is that we made it through. When God's answer for Lisa came, it was exactly right. The transition had given us a chance to let go of unrealistic expectations. We had learned what agencies and jobs worked and which ones didn't. Everything that happened in our transition time made us recognize God's timing. Prayer kept me from acting in desperation and out of sync with God's answers. Lisa achieved another important link in her lessons about trusting God. He is present in every transition. His very presence announces there is hope ahead.

Your Turn

- Understanding that parents must model what they want children to learn, identify a transition time in your life. Use Phil. 4:8 to describe what perspective you want to model during transition.
- Apply the confess-address-progress model to a transition or growth issue in your own life. Think about a time it was difficult to be honest with God or hear His truth about you. Use this understanding to pray for your child as he or she deals with similar issues.
- Using Col. 2:2, list some specific ways you can encourage the heart of your child, promote unity, and increase understanding of who God is. After you pray about your list of ideas, ask God to draw your attention to the one He wants you to act on. Report the results here.
- What is your greatest fear about this transition for your child? For you? Write a prayer based on 1 John 4:18, asking God to love fear right out of you.

I pray also that the eyes of your heart may be enlightened in order that you may know the hope to which he has called you, the riches of his glorious inheritance in the saints.

—Eph. 1:18

My Prayer

Dear God,

She's facing one of the most important decisions of her life. I fear she's leaning toward a choice that will result in unnecessary consequences. But she won't listen to me. What can I do?

Out of Control

Dear Out of Control,

Let me control *you*.

Don't let fear take my place in your life.

The God in Control

5

Praying Through Critical Times

Satan trembles when he sees
The weakest saint upon his knees.
—William Cowper

A teenage daughter with new independence starts dating someone who has the potential to influence her away from God. An adult son calls to say that he and his wife are getting a divorce. Your kindergartener comes home in tears because of teasing at school. The principal called to tell you that your fourth grader was caught stealing.

Prayer becomes an important lifeline when our children experience critical times. A critical time may not be rebellion. It may have nothing to do with spiritual failure. Instead, it may represent a time when your child feels out of control or faces the unfairness of life. It's critical because it offers a chance to apply what a child knows about God. It's where the Sunday School stories and scriptures must connect to real life in order for your child to grow and mature.

God, I bring each wounded child to Thee.
—Sarah Adams

Why Pray for Critical Times?

1. Critical times are crossroad times.

A crossroad presents choices. It could be a choice between

God-pleasing ways and God-rejecting ways. It could be a choice between good, better, and best. Making responsible choices is part of growing up. We pray for critical times because they are opportunities for growth. However, the crossroads of our children also present choices for us as parents. Our words, actions, and reactions either help our children discover how to make right choices, or they push our children away. Everyone at this crossroads needs prayer.

> *Lord,*
>   *You know the emotions of our lives, how devastating rejection is. I pray that you, our Heavenly Father, would reach out to our son during this time of hurt and rejection. Find a way to calm the storm, and hold him steady while the pieces fall about him. Draw him to you so that he finds comfort in your counsel and care. Talk to him when he needs to hear you most, and may he realize that life will not make sense without your love.*
>   *Trusting you,*
>   *A concerned father*
>   *C. Neil Strait*

2. Critical times encourage questions about God and Christianity.

Sometimes these are uncomfortable questions. When one of your child's friends dies unexpectedly, he or she may ask, "Why didn't God do something?" When a much-wanted goal or relationship crumbles, a child asks, "Why didn't God make it happen?" Critical times are not about answering all the questions. Few of us can do that. Instead, they're about helping your child discover the character of God in a new circumstance.

3. Critical times frighten us.

The danger in critical times is that they fill us with fear. We know only too well how high the stakes are. We're afraid our children will make a wrong choice or get discouraged and give up. However, if we pray out of fear, we paralyze ourselves in a way that makes it difficult to hear what God wants *us* to do.

Pray, and let God worry.
—Martin Luther

Fear prevents us from being the instruments God calls us to be. Instead, we need to learn to refocus *away* from the circumstances that produce fear and *toward* our God, who knows more about this time than we do. It doesn't mean we can get rid of fear. However, to be intercessors for our children, we need to be filled more by God than by fear.

> What are some critical issues your children face? Is it a decision, relationship, or a job? As you list them, remind yourself that there's nothing God does not know about each critical issue. With each issue, let God's knowledge and power replace any fear.
>
> _____
>
> _____
>
> _____
>
> _____
>
> _____

What We Can't Do

If we're learning anything through this journey in prayer, it's that it's not the words of our prayers that make a difference—it's always *God* who makes the difference. Our prayers won't change the nature of gravity. If a child loses his or her balance, gravity will take over. However, a child who listens to God could be directed away from a crumbling cliff. Our prayers won't change a son or daughter's mind. However, our God can help us choose the right words so that we can communicate whatever will help our child choose best. As we begin to see prayer less and less as some way to convince God of what He *needs* to do and more and more as a way to hear what God *wants us* to do; we will confront the power of prayer.

Prayer is not an argument with God to persuade him to move things our way, but an exercise by which we are enabled by his Spirit to move ourselves his way.

—Leonard Ravenhill

True prayer connects us to the mind of God. We pray to hear His mind so that we can do His work. True prayer also connects us to the *heart* of God. We perceive in deeper ways that God never ceases to love and guide. We pray that God's heart will live in us so that we can reach out in love. True prayer is our lifeline to truth and reality. We pray to recognize it, especially when it conflicts with our perspective.

The Best Way to Pray

So many times we come to God about a critical issue in the lives of our children and feel helpless to phrase our prayer in a way that will make a difference. While we may know what we want to happen, we don't know how to pray so that it will. That confusion becomes an obstacle to the peace that's to come from prayer. Of course, there are times when God confirms that what you're praying for is His heart's desire as well. But what do you do if you don't know how to pray or what to pray? Rom. 8:26 reminds us that we can rely on God's Holy Spirit to pray for us. John 14:26 tells us that the Holy Spirit will remind us of Jesus' words. These two reminders tell me that if I'm praying God's Word, I can always be sure of praying God's mind and heart.

One way to pray specifically without the danger of praying your own wants and will is to pray scripture. God's Word clearly and specifically identifies everything a child of God needs in order to make decisions that please God or persevere during grief, pain, or difficulty. Reading God's Word helps us keep God's will

---

Good Prayer Counsel

What does Rom. 8:26 tell us that the Holy Spirit will do for us? _____

_____

_____

What does John 14:26 and 16:13 say that the Holy Spirit will do for us? _____

_____

What does this teach you about prayer? _____

_____

---

as a priority. What is God's will for our children? Before anything else, it's that they belong to Him and live under His leadership.

> *Lord,*
>   *You understand how traumatic a move is for our children. As we make this move that takes them away from their friends, will you fill that void with your love, understanding, and grace? Would you bring new friends into their lives who will embrace them and welcome them and encourage them during lonely times? Help our children choose new friends who will enrich their lives and please you.*
>   *To the God who does not move,*
>   *A trusting father*
>   *C. Neil Strait*

Praying scripture is an exercise by which you identify a key scripture that fits the critical issue your child faces. Then you simply insert the name of your child into that scripture. Praying scripture protects you from praying about side issues. Instead, scripture always goes to root issues and matters of the heart.

For this critical issue . . .	Pray this scripture
A difficult decision	Rom. 1:5
Unfair or confusing circumstances	Rom. 8:31
Peer pressure or negative influences	Rom. 12:2
Ignoring or denying realities or consequences	Eph. 1:18
Listening to the wrong voices	Col. 2:8
Questions about God	Job 42:2
Confusion about the way to go	James 1:5

Pray the Lord's Prayer

I've also found the prayer that Jesus taught His disciples is a prayer that covers a variety of issues in the lives of our children. It focuses on the right priorities and the right petitions. Consider it a model for your prayers for your children. Pray it regularly for them.

- Pray that your child's attitudes and actions will honor God's name.
- Pray for your child to make God's kingdom a priority in his or her life.
- Pray for your child to seek and obey God's will.
- Pray that your child will find complete satisfaction through what God provides.
- Pray fpr your child to seek forgiveness from God or others.
- Pray that your child will turn away from temptations.

Just Ask

God says in James 1:5 that if we need wisdom—and what parent doesn't?—all we have to do is ask for it. We can ask God what His prayer is for our children, no matter what the issue is. When we stop asking for what we want and ask God to help us

Using the Lord's Prayer as your model, write a prayer for your children (Matt. 6:9-13).

Now go back and pray it specifically for yourself.

see what *He* wants, we begin to pray in different ways and with a different passion.

I remember a time when Lisa was having an especially difficult time in one of her classes. She described what happened at school in ways that made me think she may have been wronged or misunderstood. Everything in me wanted to march over to the school and tell the teacher what she didn't understand. Instead, I took the matter to God the next morning. I asked Him what I didn't know about the situation and what I should pray for. As I searched scriptures to pray, my eyes found Isa. 50:7:

> *Because the Sovereign LORD helps me, I will not be disgraced. Therefore have I set my face like flint, and I know I will not be put to shame.*

I had never used this verse to pray for anyone. However, that morning I could not get away from this verse. So I prayed it for

Lisa. I prayed that God would help her not to be disgraced or experience shame. Suddenly, like an unexpected clearing on a foggy day, I recognized the real problem Lisa faced. It wasn't unfair treatment or even misunderstanding. Lisa felt embarrassed about what she didn't know. It was one of those very clear moments when I didn't even have to ask whether this thought was correct. I knew that God had revealed the real issue. When Lisa came home that afternoon, we talked about what *really* happened. When I asked her if she had been embarrassed, she began to cry. God enabled me to see the real need and be able to help her work on some misunderstandings about her own perceptions. Real growth happened that day because God's Word directed me how to pray.

---

*Therefore be clear minded and self-controlled
so that you can pray.*

—1 Pet. 4:7

Before you pray:

1. Make sure your heart is clear before God.

Ps. 66:18 reminds us, "If I had cherished sin in my heart, the Lord would not have listened." In his book *Prayer Partners*, John Maxwell reverses this verse for a companion principle. He writes, "If I had cherished sin in my heart, *I would not have listened* to the Lord" (*emphasis mine*). How true is that? Clear hearts hear God best.

2. Reconcile your heart with your child.

Reconciling your heart with your child is especially important for adolescent and adult children. Have angry words created distance? Have you acted out of fear instead of as God's representative? Remember the foundational prayer principle that Jesus taught in Matt. 5:23-24.

If you are offering your gift at the altar and there remem-

ber that your brother has something against you, leave your
gift there in front of the altar. First go and be reconciled to
your brother; then come and offer your gift.*

Read this verse using "prayer" for "gift," and "child" for "brother." If possible, and God directs, go to your child. Take responsibility for *your* attitudes and actions. Ask forgiveness for anything that
does not represent God's character. If distance or estrangement
makes it difficult to reach out in person, confess these things to
God to clear *your* heart. This isn't about whether or not you love
your child. This is about loving your child with the love of God
himself. This is about making sure guilt, resentment, anger, or
pain doesn't create emotional obstacles for *you* as you pray.

3. Find a biblical principle that speaks to this issue.

The Bible speaks clearly about issues that could separate us
from God's ways. It shares timeless truth and foundational principles. As you seek to pray for a child at a critical time, use a
biblical principle to help focus your prayer. While the Bible
doesn't speak specifically to dating, there are plenty of verses
that speak about God-pleasing relationships. The Bible won't
tell you whether your son should get the job with the computer
company or the insurance company; it does make very clear
what a God-pleasing job is supposed to bring into life. Pray the
principles first. Let the biblical principles shape the specifics of
circumstantial prayers.

When you pray . . .

1. Pray for discernment.

Discernment is the ability to choose between good and best.
Spiritual discernment is the ability to choose what pleases God.
Do you see how both parents and children need this prayer at a
critical time? The parent can pray for discernment to seek God's
way to confront, encourage, comfort, or discipline. A child can
pray for the discernment to choose what pleases God. Learning
to discern is an important take-away skill from difficult times. As
you pray for your own spiritual discernment, you'll pray more
compassionately for the spiritual discernment of your child.

A Prayer for Discernment

Use the following verses to create a prayer for discernment.
Pray for yourself first. Then pray for your children.
1 Kings 3:9
Prov. 3:21
Phil. 1:9-10

_____

_____

_____

_____

_____

_____

_____

_____

_____

_____

_____

_____

_____

---

2. Pray that you understand the core issues.

It's easy for us to let side issues distract us. Often parents use
their energies to address the symptoms of a problem without
touching the core issues. Ask God to protect you from doing this.
Ask Him to show you the difference between the symptoms of a
problem and the real problem. A child suffering rejection may
need to understand his or her own unfriendly or annoying habits.
Simply making a child feel better is a quick fix to a deeper problem. Besides, the next time it happens, it will probably be worse.

3. Pray that your child will want God's will.

Acts 22:14 says, "The God of our fathers has chosen you to
know his will." That reminds us that the answer to our prayer is
not *our* best thought—it's *God's* thought. As you pray, make

sure that your choices and responses spring from God's will. Pray that God fills your child with a hunger for His will (Matt. 5:6). Pray that your child seeks the knowledge of God's will (Col. 1:9). Sometimes a child rejects God's will because he or she doesn't fully understand it. Pray that your child understands the true characteristics of God's will. Make sure everything you say and do contributes to what God wants your child to understand about His will.

Heb. 13:20-21 is another passage that helps me when I'm praying for God's will for another person. It reminds me that "The God of peace [will] equip you with everything good for doing his will." Nothing is more exciting than to hear the victory testimonies from a person who obeyed God's will. That choice always leads to victory. Pray that your child will obey God's will and experience God's victory.

4. Pray that your child will understand the character of God in a deeper way.

When someone rejects God's will, he or she also rejects some part of God's character. That person sees God as someone He isn't. What characteristic of God does your child need to know better so that he or she will trust that God really does know best—that He really does love better and deeper than anyone? Pray to the God who knows everything about your child (Ps. 139). Be confident that God will use all He knows about your child to fashion a one-and-only plan that will bring about good things. Rehearse the characteristics of God. Pray that your child will recognize them through this difficult time.

But now that you know God—or rather are known by God—how is it that you are turning back to those weak and miserable principles? Do you wish to be enslaved by them all over again?

—Gal. 4:9

---

5. **Pray with faith.**

Faith is about the resources of God. Faith is not about your effort. Faith is about focusing on God and His way as the end result of all prayer. Faith is not about focusing on any circumstance as the end result.

Most of us have tried to take confidence from Jesus' words in Matt. 21:21-22:

> *If you have faith and do not doubt . . . you can say to this mountain, "Go, throw yourself into the sea," and it will be done. If you believe, you will receive whatever you ask for in prayer.*

Perhaps we have misunderstood this verse and placed too much emphasis on moving the mountain and less emphasis on what real prayer is. Real prayer puts all faith in God and His character. It's not a mustering of everything in *you*. Rather, it's connecting to everything in God. That kind of connection always produces faith. Pray toward that truth, and pray because of it.

Are you praying with faith?

1. Do you believe that God has the resources to deal with this critical issue?
2. Does praying about this bring you closer to an awareness of who God is?
3. Do you believe that whatever God does is best, even if it isn't what you wanted or expected?

---

6. **Whatever you pray for your child, ask God for the same thing in your life.**

Are you praying for spiritual protection for your child? Where do you need this same protection in your life? Are you praying that your child will identify and obey God's will? Where is God asking you to identify and obey His will? When you ask God to teach *you* where you need the same prayer, you'll be able to respond more compassionately to your child as he or she struggles with the critical issue that has surfaced.

When a Child Chooses Unwisely

Your child is at some point going to choose unwisely. Maybe he or she will postpone an important school assignment and face an all-night marathon. Maybe you see warning signs about a new friend. Or maybe he or she is facing the long-term results from wrong choices. A teenager becomes a single mom. Your son seriously injures another in a car crash because he was drinking. How do you pray when the choice has been made and there are long-term consequences because of it?

First, take yourself and your heartache to God. He can't help you *feel* better about a wrong choice. That's rationalization or denial. However, He can remind you that His reaching love for your child is as strong as ever. He can remind you how you can cooperate with His plan. After bringing your own need to God, you'll be better prepared to pray for your child. Here are some ways you can pray:

- Pray that your child will recognize the difference between unwise choices and sinful choices.
- Pray for protection during a time of disobedience or delayed obedience.
- Pray that your child will ask for and accept God's strength to endure difficult consequences. Make sure you cooperate with God's plan before removing or reducing the effects of a consequence.
- Ask God to use the consequences to teach your child the wisdom of following His way.

What We Don't Know

We parents often feel fairly omniscient regarding our children. We know their personalities, their strengths, their weaknesses, their experiences. It's a humbling part of the parenting journey to recognize that God knows more about them than we do. Part of parenting involves surrendering what we know about our children to God so that He can tell us what we *need* to know. As we do that, we have to accept that we can't know everything, nor will God tell us everything. In fact,

- **God will reveal the details of His will to the person who needs to obey it.**

We know what God's will says about forgiveness, salvation, honesty, sexual morality, stewardship, and a number of other areas. However, when it comes to the right job, the right house, the right school, and so on, we may perceive a legitimate way that fulfills the requirements of God's expressed will in Scripture. But God doesn't promise to tell us what another person needs to do—even when we're the parents. He is a God of direct communication and will speak for himself. Our responsibility is to encourage our children to have direct communication with Him.

There's one exception we find in Scripture. God uses another person as His spokesman when He knows that it's the *only* way that person will hear God. Once God even used a donkey! Most of the time He used a prophet or apostle. It's not that God won't use a parent—it's just that a parent is often too close. Understanding this keeps you where you can do the most good, encouraging your child to hear God and modeling this in your own life.

This doesn't mean that God won't confirm His will for a child to parents. He will give you as much information as you will obey. *Your* obedience, not your child's, is the checkpoint. That understanding leads to another very important point:

- **To strengthen your prayers, strengthen your obedience.**

Nothing draws you to the heart of God like obedience. Obedience opens your heart to hear more from God. Your obedience to God protects you from wearing blinders during your child's difficult time. Obedience helps you understand the power of God as nothing else will. And that's what you need to know when you're praying through a difficult time in your child's life.

Do They Know You're Praying?

I'm convinced that part of the power of prayer is released when we tell someone that we're praying for him or her. When Lisa tells me about a difficult issue in her life, my first response is to brainstorm problem-solving options and give her more information. I'm learning to back away from that as my first response, and I'm learning to tell her that I'll pray for her. I can hear a certain release in her voice when I do. Depending on the issue, sometimes we just stop and pray right then.

Of course, there are some relationships in which this openness about prayer is more difficult or even impossible. Don't talk about praying for your child as a way to preach a message. Communicate your desire to pray as if you were wrapping your child in the softest comforter you can find—because that's what you're doing.

The best way to share that you're praying for your child is to make it a part of the noncritical times first. If your child is young, let the words you send him or her off to school with be "I'll be praying for you." If your teenager is having a bad day, simply say, "I'm not sure what will make it better, but I'll pray for you." For an adult child who is leaving for vacation, "I'll pray for smooth transportation and relaxing days." Just make sure they're not empty promises to pray. *Really* pray.

Lean and Learn

Critical issues make all of us aware of our need for someone who knows more than we do. As difficult as they are, sometimes these issues give us new reasons to lean on and learn about God. No parent enjoys watching his or her child experience the pain and inequality of this world; but they're inevitable. Each critical issue has the potential of drawing your child that much closer to God's will and heart. Pray with that focus and passion. Be less concerned about the specifics of the circumstances and more concerned with connecting to God himself. God will make the critical difference in the life of one who asks for His help. That promise is for you, the parent, as well as for your child.

Praying Through Critical Times

1. Clear your heart with God and with your child (Ps. 66:18).

2. Pray a biblical principle before addressing a circumstance.
3. Pray scripture, especially the Lord's Prayer (Matt. 6:9-13).
4. Pray for discernment and to understand core issues (1 Kings 3:9).
5. Pray that your child will seek God's will (Matt. 5:6).
6. Pray that your child will understand the character of God in a deeper way (Gal. 4:9).
7. Pray with faith (Matt. 21:21-22).
8. Whatever you pray for your child, ask God for the same thing in your life.
9. To strengthen your prayer, strengthen your obedience (John 14:13-15).

Your Turn

- Before you pray for your child, pray for yourself. Use Ps. 66:18 to ask God to confront anything in you that would prevent listening to Him. Pray Ps. 23—24, asking God to test your anxious thoughts and evaluate every motive. Make sure that *your* heart is cleared to hear from God.
- Use the following verses in the Psalms to review the resources of God to deal with a time of difficulty:
    Ps. 46:1-3
    Ps. 103:13-14
    Ps. 107:28-29
    Ps. 142:3
    Ps. 147:5
- Write a response to God that affirms His ability to deal with this difficulty.
- In what areas of your life do *you* need to obey God today?

Strengthen the feeble hands, steady the knees that give way; say to those with fearful hearts . . . your God will come.
—Isa. 35:3-4

Dear God,

We thank you for the privilege to be cocreator with you. We're overwhelmed by the responsibility for raising this child you have given us. Words stumble over each other as we try to express our gratitude. You have blessed us deeply. How can we thank you?

Grateful parents

Dear Grateful,

Pass my blessing on to your children.

Your First Parent

6
Praying Blessings and Affirmations

*The most eloquent prayer is the prayer
through hands that heal and bless.*
—Billy Graham

It's a miracle every time it happens. A tiny human form, curled safely inside a woman's body, makes a life-changing journey to join the outside world. You're new parents. You welcome this helpless mix of joy and responsibility with a variety of emotions. Mostly you just say, *Thank you*, as you cuddle this amazing armful of humanity at its most innocent stage.

How quickly emotions rise and fall! Fast-forward two years or thirteen. Gratitude is probably not the first emotion that comes to mind when children reorganize your schedule, manipulate your emotions, challenge every bit of self-control, and make you question your sanity. However, it's crucial to cultivate a spirit of gratitude on the difficult days. While it's not appropriate to thank God for negative circumstances or rebellious attitudes, it's always possible to thank Him for the miracle of life and the potential He planted within each child. Rehearsing your original gratitude returns you to the eternal issues involved. How do you cultivate an attitude of gratitude that does not depend on positive circumstances or cooperative children? One answer is to pray a blessing.

What Is a Prayer of Blessing?

A blessing is a statement or prayer that pronounces God's favor on another. It verbalizes what God has already said is His will for another person. It's not asking for something miraculous to come to pass in your child's life or for something to change. Actually, we don't have the power to bless another person. All we can do is ask that God will bring His blessing to someone for whom we pray.

A blessing is an extension of God's character and resources. It focuses more on who God is and what He stands for than on what you want from Him. Because of who God is, you ask Him to share the gifts of His character and resources with your child. They're gifts of protection, provision, and salvation expressed from our God, who is all power, all wisdom, and always present.

The Bible is full of God's blessings. Often they start with the words "May the Lord" followed with what a person asks of God. Each request anchors to the character of God. It's not simply a wish for good things. When tied to God's character, it's a prayer that God desires to answer in the life of your child.

Biblical Prayers of Blessing

As you read each of the following biblical blessings, identify the character trait of God that the prayer invokes:

May the LORD keep watch between you and me when we are away from each other (Gen. 31:49). _____

_____

May the LORD your God be with you (2 Sam. 14:17). _____

_____

May the LORD now show you kindness and faithfulness (2 Sam. 2:6). _____

_____

May the LORD answer you when you are in distress (Ps. 20:1).

_____

May the Lord direct your hearts into God's love and Christ's
perseverance (2 Thess. 3:5). _____

_____

May the Lord make your love increase and overflow for each
other and for everyone else, just as ours does for you
(1 Thess. 3:12). _____

May the Lord of peace himself give you peace at all times
and in every way (2 Thess. 3:16). _____

_____

Do you see how prayers of blessing are both a pronouncement and a request? These prayers acknowledge that God is
ever-seeing, always present, kind, faithful, resourceful, all loving, and the epitome of peace. It's a powerful prayer that asks
God to make your child aware of those aspects of His being. It's
productive when your child allows God to act in his or her life in
these ways. It's indeed a blessing to recognize and receive the
favor of God.

Jerry and Lynda Cohagen learned the importance of the
blessing they prayed for their first son, Chase. It became so
much a part of their bedtime ritual that, as a toddler, Chase began to rub his right ear, suck his finger, and have trouble keeping
his eyes open when the words began. At 14 months of age, he
spent five days with his grandparents. Unfortunately, the grandparents did not know about this important ritual. When Jerry and
Lynda called to find out how things were going, Grandma told
them about a strange nightly routine. As soon as she put Chase
down in his crib he kept repeating, "bessuu, keepuu." Even at 14
months of age, Chase wanted to be blessed!

The Good-Night Blessing

May God bless you and keep you
May His angels watch over and protect you.
And when you wake in the morning,
May you know you are loved.
—Jerry and Lynda Cohagen

What Is an Affirmation?

To affirm someone is to state positively and with confidence what is true. An affirmation is not necessarily a prayer. However, it can turn into a prayer when you ask God to help your child accept and recognize the truths of the affirmation.

Affirmations have more to do with personhood than behavior. They help you identify your child's essential creation by God as well as God-given characteristics and skills. In a society that often is more behavior-oriented in its parenting skills, it's very important to learn how to positively and confidently state what's true about your child—no matter how he or she behaves.

This was very difficult for me to learn as a parent, especially coming out of some of the behavior modification teaching models I studied in undergraduate and graduate work. I knew how to throw on compliments and positive statements after Lisa obeyed and cleaned her room. I did not know how to affirm her spirit separate from the way she behaved. I had to make a list of affirmations and consciously work to verbalize them during the week. My first list identified Lisa's contagious smile, sensitive spirit, and carefree giggle. Slowly, I graduated to her joyful addition to our world, her ability to help me see things for the first time or in a different way, her playful freedom. The more affirming statements I looked for, the more I found. I came to understand that affirming Lisa poured a healing balm on her spirit. It wasn't about pleasing me or obeying me. It was about my understanding of who Lisa really was.

The Affirmation Bank

Write ten affirmations for each of your children.

Name

1.

2.

3.

4.

5.

6.

7.

8.

9.

10.

Check off an affirmation after you deliver it. Every week make a new list of five more affirmations, and deliver them. Option: Do this for your spouse as well.

Is it ever possible to run out of affirmations about a person God created?

Why These Prayers Are Important

1. We live in a negative society.

It's sad that television offers us a comedy model that bases its humor on what is negative about another person. It's even worse when broken commandments become the foundation for humor. Negativism consumes our children at school with casual curses and accusations. When there are more negative models than positive, our work is doubly hard.

2. It takes ten positive words to counteract one negative word.

Ten positive words to counteract one negative word? That's probably a low estimate, but it makes us realize how much power negative words have in a person's life. Do you realize how many positive words our children need to hear from us in order to counteract the damage of the negative words they hear at work or school? Do whatever it takes to make your home a safe place where positive words of affirmation and blessing help your children heal and grow in their spirits. If your child is no longer living at home, make every effort to be generous with affirmations in every communication.

This does not mean you should excuse bad behavior. But it does provide boundaries for addressing disobedient, disrespectful, or harmful behavior. Always affirm some God-given quality about a child's personhood when disciplining. Make sure your words clearly discipline without adding to the child's negative word bank.

To Chase

Dear Chase, God blesses us with you today,
And in this gift we see again His face.
For you are love become flesh to say
That God still shows to us His love and grace.

Within our home we'll build a fortress strong
To withstand all the gales and storms about.
"Love always shall remain" will be our song
To cast out all your fears and banish doubt.

God has entrusted us with you, And so
For wisdom we will call upon His name.
In every situation may you know
Forever home and mercy are the same.

And this will be our prayer for you, dear son,
That God and you shall always walk as one.
—Lynda Cohagen

3. Positive words of blessings and affirmation are great change agents.

The more a child hears an affirmation, the more he or she will believe its truth. Saying it doesn't make it true. Rejecting it doesn't make it untrue. However, the truths of affirmations and the hopes of blessings can't release their gifts unless accepted. The courage to grow and change often comes as a child hears what someone else believes to be true about his or her personality, skills, and future. Share your blessings and affirmations as the change agent you're called to be as a parent.

4. We live in a blaming society.

Affirmations and blessings help us break the blaming cycle. You cannot bless and blame at the same time. You can't accuse and affirm at the same time. The very nature of affirmations and blessings push you to a different vocabulary to express truths and positive understandings. Get very comfortable with this kind of vocabulary in your family. Everybody needs it.

An Important Lesson

I learned an important lesson about affirmations from Anne Ortlund in her book *Children Are Wet Cement*. It was a difficult time for Lisa and me as we were just beginning our journey as mother and daughter. She had just been diagnosed with juvenile rheumatoid arthritis, and it was my arduous responsibility to help her complete a set of painful exercises two times a day. In order to get the most therapeutic value from the exercises, it was important that she relax. But Lisa couldn't relax arms and legs that hurt with each move. I struggled beyond my point of frustration to get her to do the right thing. I was full of description and criticism and definition and don'ts. None of it was helping. Then I read about affirmations from Anne Ortlund, who helped me see that I was telling Lisa everything she *wasn't* doing instead of affirming what was true. I changed my approach. Instead of looking for right behavior, I affirmed her willingness, her trying to understand, her cooperation. I found myself using more phrases like "You're doing it. That's the way." I found out that affirming her *before* achievement encouraged more progress. It was easier on *both* of us.

Praying Affirmations

List five characteristics of your children's personhood. Make sure they're true—regardless of behavior.

Name					
1.					
2.					
3.					
4.					
5.					

Confess your inability to see these characteristics as regularly as you need to. Ask God to help you see the essential personhood of your child, separate from the way he or she may use those characteristics.

Set an affirmation goal.

Example: One a day. Always after school. First thing in the morning. _____

_____

Find a verse that shows that God wants to use that characteristic for good in your child's life. Pray that verse regularly for your child.

Examples: Col. 3:12; Eph. 6:10

_____

_____

_____

The Gratitude Attitude

One of the byproducts of praying blessings and affirmations is that you develop an attitude of gratitude. Either you thank God for the limitless resources of His power and character to act on behalf of your child, or you simply find more reasons to be grateful for your child. Continuing to thank God for your children is a blessing in itself. Making it a habit prepares the foundation for listening to God and your children when circumstances are not easy.

1. Thank God for your children daily.

During the routine tasks of parenthood, thank God for the child He has given you. When gratitude is a routine response, it will make it easier to ask for and receive God's wisdom in the difficult times. Gratitude molds your perspective and helps you to focus on what is best rather than what is difficult.

2. Make a *thank list,* or start a *gratitude journal.*

On some days it's easier than others to express your gratitude. Use those times to make your list or write in your journal. As you encounter new parenting privileges, take time to record your thanks. Then, when parenting responsibilities challenge your ability to experience gratitude, take time to read the list and remind yourself of realities that don't change just because of difficulties.

Thank You, God

Start a thank-you list or write a thank-you note to God for your children. Continue to add reasons for thanks.

3. Pray and say your thanks.

Praying your thanks should be a rehearsal so that you can say thanks to your children. Children need to hear you affirm them. They need to hear it many times every day. It needs to go past thanking them for doing good things. Finish this sentence several times a day: "You are so _____." Resourceful, maybe? Happy? Creative? Look for new ways to express your awareness. Leave a note on the pillow. Tuck a message in the lunchbox. Hide it where you know your child will find it. Watch the glow on your child's face when he or she experiences the healing effects of such positive expressions.

4. Express your thanks and affirmations in public.

Brag on your children. Don't overdo it to the point of embarrassment. Just express some of these affirmations to other people when they're around. Remember—it's not bragging on what they *do*. That can set up a standard hard to live up to. It's all about affirming who they *are*.

Lord,

These are my beautiful children. You have been so good to give them to me. I thank you for them and the joy they give us. I ask for guidance to be the example they need to see. When I make mistakes, help me to be big enough to say so. More than anything, Lord, I want to be a good parent, for I know they're gifts from you. Help me to grow as the parent you created me to be. Help me to show you to our children and to teach them your ways. Help me to live and say the gratitude that fills my heart.

> *Thanking you,*
> *A very grateful parent*
> *Ina Strait*

Scriptural Blessings

The Beatitudes (Matt. 5:3-11) pronounce God's favor on those who adopt God-pleasing discipleship standards in their lives. For example, praying that your child be "poor in spirit" isn't about having no money or being depressed or discouraged. It's about understanding how poor and helpless we are without the Lord. It's about understanding that God wants to bless each life with the riches of his redemption.

The Jabez blessing in 1 Chron. 4:10 has received a lot of attention because of Bruce Wilkinson's book. It's a prayer for God's provision and protection. It helps those who pray it to look for the opportunities God tucks into life.

Perhaps the most used prayer of blessing in the Bible comes from Num. 6:24-26: "The LORD bless you and keep you; the LORD make his face shine upon you and be gracious to you; the LORD turn his face toward you and give you peace." Choirs sing it, and pastors end Sunday worship with it. It embodies all of what we need from God to live a productive and God-pleasing week.

The Children's Blessing

May God bless you.
May you hear the voice of Christ
And respond to His voice.
May God keep your heart open and tender toward God.
May you learn how much He loves you.
And may you spend the rest of your life
responding to God's love.
—Debbie Goodwin

Bless Them

When you don't know what else to pray for your child, pray a blessing. No one can have too many blessings. Gather a group of other parents and commit to simply praying blessings for your children. Talk about the ways it helps you see where God is at work in your child's life as well as in your own. Celebrate the discoveries you find as you look for new understandings about your children. Blessings are positive prayers. They are freeing prayers. Nothing settles a heart more than a prayer of blessing. Learn to pray them often. You'll come to recognize this form of prayer as a good way to celebrate the life stages of your children and connect them to the resources of God. Consider writing prayers for birthdays, the beginning of school, the beginning of summer, dating, marriage, first child. The possibilities are endless. So is the favor of God. That's the greatest blessing. May you discover it for yourself and for your children.

Praying Blessings and Affirmations

1. A blessing pronounces God's favor on your children.
2. A blessing is an extension of God's character.
3. An affirmation states positively what is true.
4. Affirm a child based on personhood and not behavior.
5. A by-product of blessings and affirmations is gratitude.

Your Turn

- Begin with a scriptural promise. Many parents use Jer. 29:11, Phil. 4:19, or even Ps. 23. How can you turn it into a prayer of blessing?
- Combine an affirmation (pronouncement of personhood) with a blessing (pronouncement of God's favor). Use the following examples to get you started: Phil. 1:9-11, 1 Sam. 23:21, 25:33, 2 Sam. 2:4-6.
- Turn scripture into a prayer of blessing by introducing it with "May the Lord . . ." Try this with 1 Cor. 1:5-9.

I have received a command to bless . . .
and I cannot change it.
—Num. 23:20

Dear God,

We are in awe of your work in our children's lives. You have rescued, restored, strengthened, loved, healed, forgiven, empowered, and transformed. We are front-row witnesses to your power and creativity. What can we do to make sure it continues?

Completely Humbled

**Dear Humbled,
Never stop praying.**

**The God Who
Answers**

7
Never Stop Praying

*Heaven is full of answers to prayer for which
no one ever bothered to ask.*
—Billy Graham

If prayer really makes a difference, no parent should start a day without it. If God really desires an ongoing conversation with us about the children He has loaned us, then we should prevent any obstacle or distraction from hearing His instructions. If we are God's representatives to His children, then everything should send us to our knees.

―――――――

*Prayer is the helpless cry of someone who
understands that his or her only hope is God.*
—Mark Goodwin

―――――――

Prayer is not a ritual or some formula of special words. It's a most intimate connection with the heart of the Creator. We become present to God so that He shares His presence with us. Yes, we can pour out our hearts and ask for specific things. But prayer is more than a cathartic emptying of emotional stress. It's more than our heart's deepest wish list. Through prayer, God, Creator of the balance and intricacies of our world, speaks to us about what He knows. He shares the one step that begins an answer. He always gives us something to obey, because He knows how hard it is for us to do nothing. It usually isn't what we expect. It often is a step of surrender. It's that surrender that changes us. It's that surrender that enables us to be instruments of His will in the lives of our children.

Pray First

Learn to pray first. Pray before giving the lecture. Pray before deciding on the discipline. Pray before making the threat you don't want to keep. Pray first. If you let Him, God will help you identify the key issues at stake. He will help you know how to make the right kind of difference.

Ways to Pray for Your Children

1. Purchase a Bible. Read through it, dating and underlining every scripture you pray for your children. At a significant time, present the Bible as a gift.
2. Ask your children what to pray for.
3. Find or compose special prayers to present at birthdays and special days.
4. Commit to pray for your children at a special time of the day or when you engage in a regular activity.
5. Use your children's pictures around the house to remind you to pray for them.
6. Step into a child's room when he or she is asleep. Consider kneeling at the foot of the bed to pray.
7. Step into a child's room when he or she is away. Use items in the room to help you pray for that child.
8. When separated, use something that belongs to your child as your reminder to pray for him or her. Send a symbol with your child as a prayer promise.
9. Collect prayers that help you express what you want to pray. Date them every time you use them. Let them teach you what to pray.
10. Take a prayer walk with your child. Use objects from God's world to prompt prayers of gratitude or guidance. Just stop and pray, and then resume walking.

Pray About Everything

There's nothing too insignificant to pray about. If it concerns you or your child, it's something God wants to help with. Pray about their school tests and your reaction to their grades. Pray for their teachers and your ability to cooperate with them. Pray that lunch conversation is positive and affirming. Pray for dating relationships. Pray for driving safety. Pray for them on the job, and pray for them when they're looking for work. Pray for their marriages and parenting skills. Pray that they'll find places of service and ministry in a church that helps them grow spiritually. There's always something to pray about.

Instead of worrying, pray.
—Phil. 4:6, TM

Why Worry?

Why worry when you can pray? That's the message God teaches us in His word. He tells us that we can't do anything productive or positive by worrying. Worry shrivels the soul and pushes our children away. Worry focuses on circumstances that we don't usually have any power over. Worry produces fear, not peace. It steals confidence instead of contributing to it.

Are You a Prayer *Worrier?*

When Lisa was a teenager, she participated in a small youth musical group. Donna volunteered to lead it. Lisa came home from one practice very frustrated because of the way the other teens treated Donna. We were sorry to hear about it, because we knew that Donna had received some terrifying news over the weekend. The cancer that had been in remission was back. Her future was very uncertain. We told Lisa how much Donna needed her support because of some difficult news.

Donna came to me a week later with the note Lisa had written her. In it Lisa thanked her for working with their music group. One sentence stood out. She told Donna that she wanted to be her prayer "worrier." Of course, Lisa meant prayer "warrior." How many times do we become prayer *worriers* instead of prayer *warriors*? It depends on whether we focus on God or focus on the circumstances. It depends on whether we stubbornly see only one thing or are willing to submit our finite perspective to the God who sees everything.

Praying isn't just a bookend experience, something to begin and close our day. Prayer is life. It's for busy people who don't have a quiet, sit-down time during the day. It's for those who can successfully schedule a chunk of focused time just to "be still, and know" (Ps. 46:10). There is no reason not to pray.

To become a praying parent you have to start praying. It's as simple as that. Whether you use the principles in this book or other helpful models, the important issue is that you pray—often, always, without stopping.

Can God stop you midsentence to tell you that you're saying too much to a child? He can if you've asked Him to when you pray. Your very obedience in small but often very critical moments of a day becomes your prayer. Obedience will always be more valuable than any words you can say. This means that hearing God is prayer; obeying Him is prayer. It's not about the words. It's about the heart—His and yours.

Prayer Makes a Lasting Difference

There's no way to put a price tag on the value of a praying parent in a child's life. Your attitudes and habits, your priorities and values shape your children. No one will be a perfect parent. However, everyone can be a praying parent. Prayer is the opening God wants to use to make a difference in your life and in your child's life. Make prayer your most important parenting discipline. Pray about everything. Pray every day. Pray when you don't feel like it. Pray harder when you do. Pray to the God who knows more than you do. Pray to the God whose arms of love and compassion will hold you through the worst of any parenting storm. It's not about getting some*thing* when you pray. It's about connecting to God.

Never, ever stop praying for your kids. There's no problem too big for God. No rebellion is too fierce. No truth is too ugly. No past is too horrible. There's no sin that can't be forgiven. Fall into the arms of the one who loves you and your children more than you have dared to believe. Trust His answers and His timing, no matter what you see. Make a lasting difference in the lives of your children with prayer. No matter what happens to you or to them, never, ever stop praying.

Dear God,

We present ourselves to you as parents called to be your representatives to the children you have loaned us. Examine our words and our hearts. Confront us about anything that does not represent your character. Encourage us when we feel inexperienced and incompetent. Use your loving parent ways to meet the deepest needs in our hearts and heal our most frightening hurts. Thank you for parenting us in a way that provides an ever-present model, no matter what other models we have seen. Thank you that your parenting is positive, affirming, and transformational. Make us that kind of parent with our words and actions. May we never be afraid of surrender even when it appears to cost us deeply. May we live every day with the knowledge that there's nothing you will withhold from us or our children that could make an eternal difference. Trusting that truth, may we seek often those answers from you so that our prayers become the requests you're already answering.

With all love and growing trust,
Many parents

Your Turn

- What's the most important lesson you've learned about prayer in this journey? What difference has it already made?
- Write a prayer covenant for each of your children, using the model below. Consider presenting it to them as a spe-

cial birthday or Christmas present. Each year, write an accountability report.

I covenant
   —to present myself to God for His examination before I talk to Him about you.
   —to obey anything He asks of me regarding my attitudes, words, or actions.
   —to trust you to Him, knowing that He loves you even more than I do.
   —to pray for you regularly and specifically.
   —to search the Scriptures for the prayers God wants me to pray for you.
   —to learn to pray first before speaking or suggesting or criticizing.
   —to ask you often what you want me to pray for.
   —to share with you the lessons I'm learning about prayer and how these lessons are changing me.

- Determine how you will establish a regular time to pray for your children and write it down. Recruit an accountability partner. Weekly or monthly, report your progress.
- Never stop praying.

I know that through your prayers . . . what has happened to me will turn out for my deliverance.
—Phil. 1:19

Prayer Contributors

Jerry and Lynda Cohagen: Together, Jerry and Lynda have published a family column and have written, published, and performed sketches on marriage and family. However, their most important partnership produced Chase and Tori. They continue to pray their parent prayers from Bourbonnais, Illinois, where Jerry is a professor and director of the theatre department at Olivet Nazarene University and Lynda teaches in the public high school.

Dave and Becky Le Shana: Dr. Le Shana is a former president of George Fox University, Seattle Pacific University, and Western Evangelical Seminary. He and his wife, Becky, enjoy supporting all four of their adult children in their parenting adventures. They live in Lake Oswego, Oregon, where Dr. Le Shana keeps an active schedule serving on various international and collegiate boards.

Bette Dale Moore: A valued music educator for Nampa, Idaho, public schools, Bette Dale Moore created and directs an anti-drug drama-music presentation that tours statewide. She uses her unrelenting energy to write, publish, act, and direct music and drama for her church, elementary school, university, and Community Theatre Troupe. However, nothing takes more energy or prayer than parenting her two children.

Gary Sivewright: Gary has helped numerous parents and young adults make college transition through his work as professor and chaplain at Mount Vernon Nazarene University. He and his wife, Carol, have survived the college transitions of their sons, Chad and Jason. Gary is a writer, gifted communicator, and trusted counselor. He and Carol continue to pray for their adult sons.

Stan and Linda Toler: Stan is pastor of Trinity Church of the Nazarene in Oklahoma City. He is also a prolific writer, challenging speaker, and the father of two sons. He understands the difference prayer makes. Linda, Stan's wife, teaches third grade. Well-known for his Minute Motivator series, Stan's newest releases include *The Secret Blend* and *The Cycle of Victorious Giving*.

Parenting Books
from Beacon Hill Press

"Littleton offers a ray of hope for dark times."
— **Will Penner**, editor of *Youthworker Journal*

when your teen goes astray

Help and Hope from Parents Who Have Been There

JEANETTE GARDNER LITTLETON

083-412-0445

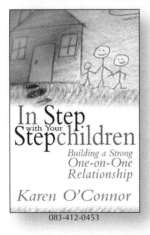

In Step with Your Stepchildren

Building a Strong One-on-One Relationship

Karen O'Connor

083-412-0453

BEACON HILL PRESS
OF KANSAS CITY

When Your Teen Goes Astray
will teach you principles to:

- Communicate with your teen

- Deal with confrontation and conflict

- Set boundaries and enforce rules

- Cope with grief, loss, and anger

- Support your spouse to form a solid parenting partnership, and much more.

In Step with Your Stepchildren
explores unique ways that stepparents can build honest, deep, lasting relationships with their stepchildren. It's not about blended families but about the one-on-one relationship between a stepparent and a stepchild, teaching stepparents how to relate to each stepchild as an individual.

Visit Your Local Christian Bookstore and Order Today!

More Parenting Books from Beacon Hill Press

083-412-0496

7 Emotional Skills Every Child Needs teaches you to nurture skills in your children that will foster intimacy in relationships. These seven skills provide a foundation for children to communicate and relate to you—the parent—and to allow children to worship God and to be intimate with Him.

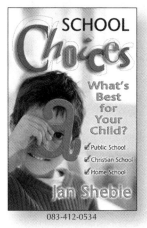

083-412-0534

School Choices helps parents choose between home schooling, private schooling, or public schooling. It gives parents tools to evaluate the quality of local public and private schools, and it gives parents who choose home schooling information on how to prepare their home, their children, and their curriculum for this challenging task.

BEACON HILL PRESS
OF KANSAS CITY

Visit Your Local Christian Bookstore and Order Today!